PERFORMANCE APPRAISAL

A Manager's Guide

C. PATRICK FLEENOR
Albers School of Business
Seattle University

M. PETER SCONTRINO
Scontrino and Associates

KENDALL/HUNT PUBLISHING COMPANY
Dubuque, Iowa

Copyright © 1982 by Kendall/Hunt Publishing Company

Library of Congress Catalog Card Number: 81-83153

ISBN 0-8403-2534-7

All rights reserved. No part of this publication may be reproduced, stored in a retrieval system, or transmitted, in any form or by any means, electronic, mechanical, photocopying, recording, or otherwise, without the prior written permission of the copyright owner.

Printed in the United States of America

B 402534 01

To

Margaret
and
Connie

Contents

Preface   vii

Chapter 1.   **Performance Appraisal: An Overview**   1
    Some Appraisal Issues   1
    People and Their Performance   3
    Use of Performance Appraisal   8
    Successful Appraisal Systems   9
    A System Perspective   11

Chapter 2.   **Selecting an Appraisal System**   13
    Goals of Performance Appraisal   13
    Some Technical Considerations   19
    Common Evaluation Systems   22
    Communicating the Goals of Your System   40
    Rating Your Organization's Appraisal System   41

Chapter 3.   **Developing Performance Criteria and Standards**   43
    Why Performance Criteria?   43
    Performance Standards   50
    Example of a Multi-purpose Performance Appraisal Form   60

Chapter 4.   **Protecting Employee Rights: Avoiding Rater Errors**   65
    Enforcement of Title VII   68
    Reliability   69
    Validity   70
    Checking for Rater Bias   72
    Common Rater Errors   75
    Halo and Horns Effect   78
    Central Tendency and Leniency   79
    Similar-to-Me Error   81
    Contrast Effect   82

Chapter 5.   **The Formal Review Session**   85
    Fear of Appraisal   86
    Interview Preparation   86
    Interview Initiation   87
    Interview Structuring   87

	Interview Communication	88
	Planning for Future Performance	103
	Interview Closing	110
Chapter 6.	**Concluding Comments**	111
	An Evaluation Checklist	113
	Training of Raters	114
	Summary	115

Appendix A: An Employee Manual   116
Appendix B: An Essay Appraisal Form   120
Appendix C: Management by Objectives and Criteria-only Form   129
Appendix D: Form Adaptable to Most Approaches   139
Appendix E: Criteria and Standards Form   151
Appendix F: Customer/Client Appraisal Form   202

Glossary   204

Bibliography   205

Preface

Books have many origins. This one stemmed from our professional frustration at the lack of a single source that would give practicing managers a complete picture of the performance appraisal process.

We work extensively with managers and our consulting experiences led to several purposes for starting the project. First, we wanted to present the appraisal process as the system it is, and to show how it relates to other aspects of management and the organization. Second, we wanted to show that performance appraisal is a logical, common-sensical extension of good management practice; not a fearsome, horrendously complex boondoggle designed to multiply the tentacles of the personnel department. Thirdly, we wanted to provide a framework for appraisal in organizations of any size and any industry, public or private. We also wanted to emphasize practicality, while using the most current theoretical concepts, supported by current research evidence. There are few footnotes or citations in the body of the book, but a very complete bibliography of empirical research and books on performance appraisal is located at the end of the book for those readers who want more background in the various aspects of appraisal. The bibliography is divided into topic areas for ease of use.

Finally, we wanted to provide some examples of good appraisal practices. To that end, we have included a number of "war stories" from our consulting experience, and a rather extensive selection of appraisal forms in the Appendix. We caution the reader that a good form does not an appraisal system make, and in fact the form is typically the *last* element of the system to be designed or selected.

This book is intended for several audiences. First and foremost among them are those practicing managers at all levels who must evaluate the performance of their subordinates. Second, we intend the book for personnel officers who desire a volume that is short, yet covers the major elements of performance appraisal. Third, this book is for use in schools or departments of business administration, public administration and educational administration. Specifically we see the book as a supplementary text in personnel management courses or in management seminars.

To avoid overly cumbersome wording we have used the generic 'he' in some places in the book to refer to a person. It should be obvious from our examples and illustrations that we do not consider all, or even most, managers to be male.

Many people and organizations contribute to the creation of any book. We would particularly like to thank our colleague, Dr. Harry Springer, for his contribution to the writing of Chapter Five.

We also appreciate the permission to reproduce the appraisal forms of a number of different organizations from the private and public sectors. Some of the forms have had the corporate names removed, by request of the organizations.

Ms. Deborah Woolley improved the readability of the manuscript significantly through her skillful editing. Ms. Joan Blanusa and Ms. Sally Olson ably deciphered our hand-written notes and arrows leading to nowhere, to produce the final draft.

Seattle, Washington   C.P.F.
                       M.P.S.

CHAPTER 1

Performance Appraisal: An Overview

Today's manager is under substantial pressure to evaluate employee performance on a more formal basis than in the past. To some, this feels like being asked to "play God," since an employee's success on the job may depend largely on the manager's evaluation.

But in spite of our general reluctance to "play God" by judging the worth of other human beings (at least in face-to-face encounters), performance appraisal is an inevitable part of managing. We do it continually—if not formally,— at least informally. Therefore the question is not "if," but "how." This book addresses the question of "how," through showing the reader ways to design performance appraisal mechanisms at the organizational, departmental and individual levels to accomplish the desired result: better employee performance.

SOME APPRAISAL ISSUES

In designing an appraisal system, the following questions and issues must be faced.[1]

THE SYSTEM

Should the *system* be based upon:

personal prejudices of the evaluator	or	performance on the job
subjective opinions	or	objective measures
personal traits and characteristics	or	job related criteria
continuing feedback	or	periodic formal statements
sweeping generalizations	or	critical incidents

---

1. We are indebted to Professor James E. Rosenzweig of the University of Washington for the issues raised in the following list.

assumptions	or	valid visible data
form	or	substance

Clearly, the system should be based upon actual job performance rather than the (usually) unstated prejudices of the evaluator. Therefore it becomes necessary to provide as many objective measures as possible. There is no such thing as a *completely* objective method for appraisal, but subjectivety should be reduced to the extent possible. Job related criteria should be evaluated rather than personal traits and characteristics like "personality" or "aggressiveness."

Employees should receive continuing feedback *supplemented* by periodic formal reviews. A once-annual discussion of performance is simply not adequate. All feedback should relate to critical (important) activities of the employee and avoid sweeping generalizations. The manager must assume as little as possible, relying instead on visible data.

Finally, we would hope that our appraisal system emphasizes real contributions rather than mere "style," and does not become so encumbered with paperwork that employees and managers miss the point entirely.

THE EMPLOYEE

Should the employees perceive performance appraisal to be:

done to them	or	done with them
pointing out fatal flaws	or	used for closing gaps
punishment for low performance	or	based upon reward for good performance
parent ⇌ child relationship	or	an adult ⇌ adult relationship
comparison to other people	or	comparison with standards

Employees should be able to view appraisal as a joint effort to improve job performance. Too many appraisal systems leave employees feeling helpless and angry. Appraisal should emphasize the closing of performance "gaps" rather than the highlighting of flaws that the employee can do nothing about.

The overall cast of appraisal should be positive, focussing on the rewards inherent in improved performance rather than dwelling interminably on the punishment awaiting any miscues. Just as do managers, employees want to be treated as adults in a mature exchange of information and ideas rather than as adolescents in need of instruction.

Certainly, people should be compared with some specific standards (that are known to all) rather than with other people.

Comparing a Honda motorcycle with a Mercedes limousine tells us little about either vehicle. We must have criteria (e.g., mileage, comfort, cost, ease of service, etc.), before we can make a judgment about which is "best." Extending the logic, it is neither fair nor sensible to compare a young, unexperienced clerk with a wise, mature program analyst in the same department. We must have standards of performance instead.

THE MANAGER

Judge	or	Counselor
Garbage collecting (time bomb)	or	Confronting performance issues

The manager cannot completely avoid the role of judge, but by virtue of the position a manager holds, there is an inherent obligation to counsel and help employees improve performance. This occurs primarily through the timely confrontation of performance issues. The manager who "collects garbage" (tabulates problems and irritations without communicating them, then delivers a "bomb" at the formal review) is an ineffective manager.

There are other issues of importance where the answer is not "either-or" as above, but "how much of each."

APPRAISAL EMPHASIS

rating or grading past performance	versus	future development
current job	versus	promotability
remedying weaknesses	versus	building on strengths
communicating	versus	understanding
uniformity	versus	unity

The relative emphasis given these poles has a direct bearing on the design and complexity of the appraisal system, as well as the time commitment required of all parties. The more uses desired, the more elaborate and costly the system will be.

PEOPLE AND THEIR PERFORMANCE

If we assumed performance to be entirely under the control of the individual to be evaluated, we would need to consider only two variables, as in Figure 1.1.

Note that performance requires both ability and motivation. Neither will substitute for the other beyond a very narrow range. No matter how highly

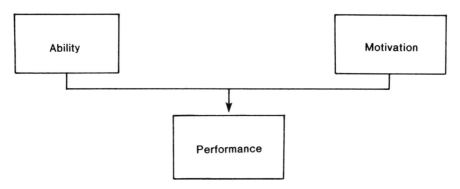

Figure 1.1. A simple model of performance.

motivated an individual, lack of ability will result in low performance. Similarly, great ability will not lead to high performance without motivation to perform. If we are blessed with able, motivated workers, we would then expect them to be high performers. However, to develop a fuller understanding of performance, we must elaborate upon both ability and motivation.

ABILITY

In Figure 1.2 we see that ability is a function of knowledge, motor skills and experience. Knowledge and motor skills are relatively easy to assess through testing devices. Lack of knowledge can easily be corrected through training, while motor skills can generally be improved somewhat through training and practice. Note that experience is a function of past performance. While experience is simple to *count*—e.g., three years at one job, four years at another—*quality* of experience is what's important. There is a vast difference in value between five years of experience with increasing levels of responsibility, and one year of experience repeated four times.

MOTIVATION

The motivation half of performance is more complex, and can be viewed as a combination of personal goals, results of past performance, and the history of past success or failure.

Personal Goals and Needs

Personal goals and needs have a profound effect upon motivation level. Some people have very ambitious personal goals that can be satisfied at least partly through performance on the job, while others appear to be drifting.

To change personal goals or needs is both technically and ethically beyond the scope of the organization. However, it can be very useful for the manager to

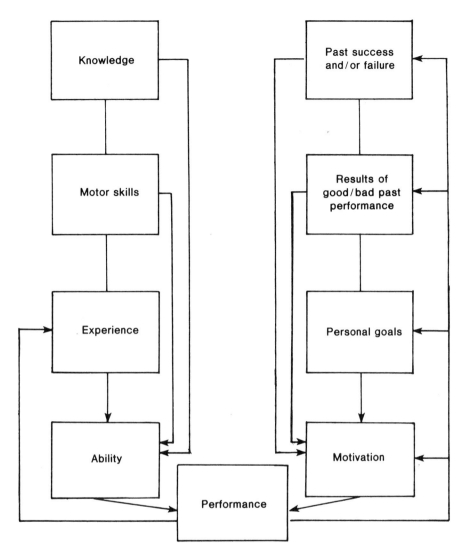

Figure 1.2. Elements of ability and motivation.

know something about each employee's personal goals since on-the-job performance will be enhanced if the task in some way supports a personal goal. For example a person who has a goal of becoming promotable and becoming more valuable to the organization is likely to be pleased with assignments of increasing challenge, even those outside the current job description. The reverse is also true of course. The employee with little attachment to the organization and no career aspirations may prefer to be treated with benign neglect.

Personal needs are also relevant. The extremely gregarious employee with a high need for affiliation might feel frustrated at spending all day researching billing data from a computer terminal, but excel in dealing with telephone queries about billing.

Though personal goals and needs cannot be changed in any real sense, they may be used to place employees in situations that will appeal to them.

Past Performance

Motivation levels are also affected by results of past performance. If good performance is ignored, and/or if poor performance is ignored, the implicit message to employees is that management is indifferent or oblivious to differences in performance levels. In many organizations there are little or no consequences related to performance. If performance feedback is rarely or never given, and all salary increases are based on seniority, then it literally makes no difference how well one performs provided that it is above the level that would result in termination.

The authors have met many employees, including managers, who have *never* had a performance appraisal—in one case, for 25 years. Good performers in such an environment are probably motivated almost entirely by their personal goals, since the organization provides precious little reason to excel.

Fast Success/Failure

Finally, the history of past success and/or failure affects motivation. People with a history of success expect to succeed in the future, and tend to work vigorously to ensure success. Those with a history of failure often expect to fail in the future, and may behave in ways that ensure failure (a kind of reverse Pygmalion effect).

THE ENVIRONMENT

Of course, individual performance does not take place in a vacuum; aspects of the working environment also impact performance.

Working conditions, availability of proper equipment and the leadership style exercised by the manager also relate to both the willingness and ability of an individual to perform. It seems obvious that uncomfortable working conditions; that are perhaps noisy, too hot or too cold, poorly lighted, crowded, etc.,

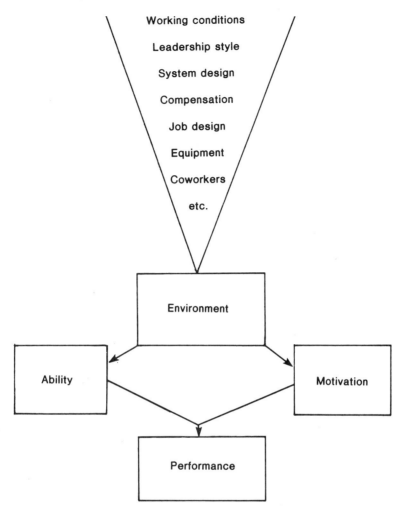

Figure 1.3. Performance in the organizational setting.

may lead to poor performance. Similarly, absence of needed equipment makes good performance difficult at the least.

Less obviously, an inappropriate supervisory style may lead to employee performance problems. The self-motivated highly competent subordinate may be offended by a supervisory style that is too structured, while a weaker employee might profit substantially from close supervision. The design of the personnel system and design of the job itself either support performance or detract from it.

Employees should see promotions, preferential assignments, etc., as stemming from good performance. The jobs must be at least tolerable, and preferably interesting before one can expect effort beyond a minimal level. Compensation and other rewards must be linked directly to performance if we want them to have any effect. The group dynamics created by co-workers can either encourage or discourage good performance. Groups define and enforce their own norms, and a work group with an antagonistic view of management will exert pressure on others to adopt the same view. The more cohesive the group and more negative the relations with management, the lower the performance of any individual in the group is likely to be. Figure 1.3 presents the complete performance model.

USE OF PERFORMANCE APPRAISAL

Performance appraisal serves many purposes in the organization:

Control

A physician knows a patient with a temperature of 102°F has "a temperature" only because there is a standard of 98.6°F for comparison. Control of the temperature may be achieved in several ways, but progress can only be assessed via comparison with the standard. If the patient's temperature continues to rise, the treatment plan is changed. If the temperature decreases the treatment plan is continued until the standard or "normal" temperature is reached.

In an organization the appraisal system defines standard or "normal," sets benchmarks for comparison and can initiate action to bring deviation from standard back into line.

Training Needs

Training gaps at both the individual and group level can be diagnosed more accurately. The existence of criteria allow both management and employees to define skill needs more specifically.

Personnel Decisions

Performance appraisal can be used to identify "fast-track" employees who are promotable, by clearly highlighting their strengths as well as pinpointing areas where skill development is desirable.

Problem performers can be spotted earlier and their *specific* deficiencies documented and corrected.

Furthermore, transfer can be made on a more logical basis, allowing the organization to place employees in positions that will capitalize on their strengths and minimize their weaknesses.

Merit pay and bonus plans take on new force when they are tied to a quality appraisal system. Obviously, merit pay should be based upon actual performance, but sadly, the connection is tenuous at best in many organizations. A good appraisal system can make the link between performance and merit compensation clear to all concerned.

Feedback

This is the bottom line. Feedback is the foundation upon which all uses of performance appraisal are constructed. Virtually every employee (including the reader, we wager) has a recurring question about his or her job. That question is: "How am I doing?" Performance appraisal should answer that question clearly, specifically, and regularly.

The system can also be used to make comparisons among raters, identifying those raters who may be unreasonably easy or hard on their employees, as well as raters who may be biased against certain individuals or groups.

SUCCESSFUL APPRAISAL SYSTEMS

The signs of a successful appraisal system are simple: it is used, it is understood, and is perceived as being honest and fair. We have seen organizations "require" performance appraisal and assume that the system is being used. However, appraisal is used only if it is useful to those involved. Filing an annual form does not necessarily mean that appraisal is being done. The users must also understand the system, so it should not be more complex than necessary. Finally, both managers and employees should see the system to be impartial. Favoritism in any form will destroy the trust that people must place in the appraisal process. Once destroyed, trust is very difficult to re-establish.

In our work with appraisal systems, we have concluded that successful systems are accompanied by some organizational conditions that lead to the desired state of usefulness.

Employee Participation

Employees should be involved in development of the system, for two reasons. First, the people actually doing the job have the most current information about the structure of that job. The criteria which will be developed as part of the system will then be job related. In some cases it is even required by law that appraisal systems be job related, an issue discussed in detail in Chapter 4. Moreover, unless the appraisal system is job related, it cannot measure what it purports to measure. Secondly, participation in the development of the system makes the appraisal process less of an unknown. Employees will understand the system if they assist in its design.

Management Support

Management, especially at the executive level, must support the appraisal system. Besides providing the tangible support of money, people and time for development, management at all levels should "model" the system. That is, they should use it themselves, as well as requiring others to use it.

In-House Expertise

If you have dealt with consultants, you know that when the consultant rides into the sunset, his/her expertise follows on the pack-horse. Immediately following that dramatic scene, unanswered questions begin popping up (e.g., how does this thing work?).

While it is not absolutely necessary that a consultant be hired to help develop your appraisal system, it may help. Consultant or no, the organization is ultimately responsible for development, but the consultant can provide needed facilitation. It is imperative that *someone* in the organization be involved in all phases of the development. It should be someone who is, or can become, knowledgable about appraisal in general and about your system in particular. If a consultant is retained, that person should work closely with the consultant. The nominee then becomes a resource within the organization, an "internal consultant" for those using the system.

Training

Too often, great attention is paid to the creation of an appraisal form which is then handed to managers with little or no explanation. Once you have devised a gorgeous, illustrated, multi-page, multi-color form, your system is complete, right? No! A performance appraisal form is not performance appraisal. The form is only that—a form. Appraisal is a process, not a piece of paper, and users of the system must understand that. Management must realize that using the form—putting it into practice as an appraisal system—requires certain skills. Supervisors need training in how to observe performance, how to fill out the form and how to give feedback. Specific training needs are discussed at greater length later in the book.

Performance Notes

One of the authors conducted a seminar for an organization that usually has several training programs running simultaneously at its large conference center. One of the programs to be offered that day was "Memory Building." About 35 people from several states had enrolled for "Memory Building." They waited patiently in the training room as the scheduled starting time came and went. Unfortunately, the seminar leader had forgotten the seminar. The seminar had to be cancelled, and presumably the trainer is now in another line of work.

The human memory is a marvelous device that ordinarily performs yeoman service. Unfortunately, memory is not reliable where it is a question of large amounts of detail over long time periods. Since it is impossible to reconstruct the performance of employees from memory, a necessary adjunct to a performance appraisal system is the accumulation of data. Periodic notations should be made about the performance of every employee. These notes became the raw data for the formal appraisal, allowing the manager to relate specific incidents of activity in support of the ratings.

Specific Performance Objectives

"Having lost sight of our objective, we immediately redoubled our efforts," is an old management aphorism to describe the confusion resulting from lack of a planning mechanism. The best appraisal systems focus on the future as well as the past, requiring supervisors and employees to agree on some objectives for the following performance review period.

Feedback

As mentioned earlier, this is the *raison d'etre* of performance appraisal. Quality feedback is a requirement, not a luxury.

A SYSTEM PERSPECTIVE

The word "system" has appeared several times already, and will be used many more times. A system is a series of interrelated parts. The term is used with performance appraisal to remind us that appraisal does not stand alone in the organization, but is related to many other things. The appraisal system can be broken down into a series of related subsystems, as below:[2]

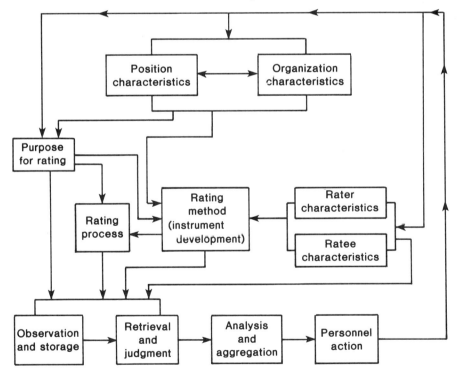

Figure 1.4. The performance appraisal system.

2. Adapted from Landy, Frank J. and James L. Farr, "Performance Rating", in *Psychology Bulletin,* 87 (1), Jan., 1980, p. 94

The context in which rating occurs is that of the particular organization. Specific features of the organization such as the number of people reporting to supervisors (span of control), rate of turnover, full-time to part employee ratio, 7–day vs. 5–day operations, number of shifts, etc. determine to some degree the methods and fequency of appraisal.

In addition, the position(s) being rated differ across many dimensions—e.g., line vs. staff, fixed location vs. mobile, complexity of tasks, measurability of output, etc. Features of the positions will determine, in part, the criteria included in the system.

Organization and position characteristics influence the choice of rating method and the purpose for rating—development, compensation decisions, counseling, training, and the like. Choice of rating method is also affected by characteristics of the rater and ratee, including variables like age, race, sex, education level, experience, and skills.

In turn, the method of rating and the purposes for which it will be used define the appraisal process: frequency of ratings, what data are shared with the ratee, whether single or multiple raters are used, etc.

All of the considerations mentioned thus far influence the thinking processes of the rater, directly or indirectly. The system as designed will determine the kinds of ratee behaviors that are observed and "stored" either in the rater's memory or in a performance diary.

For example, appraisal criteria that emphasize quantity of output will require managers to collect data related to speed and efficiency. Criteria that emphasize quality of output will require data related to carefulness and accuracy. At some point the data are retrieved and judgments on ratee performance are made. The data are then analyzed and aggregated into a performance description that will influence any personnel decisions that may follow the performance appraisal. Over time, those personnel actions may result in changes in the organization and in position characteristics, as well as in the purpose of rating.

One organization for example, reclassified a number of positions after performance criteria were developed and appraisal of employees on the criteria revealed that many of the employees were performing duties much broader than those listed in their job description.

As an integral part of the personnel system, the appraisal system must be reviewed periodically and accommodated to changing conditions. For example, a number of government agencies are implementing merit pay plans. Consistency between the various raters will become very important as merit plans are installed, and appraisal methods to encourage that consistency will have to be designed.

The ultimate purpose of performance appraisal is to enhance organization effectiveness through increased productivity at the individual and group level. In the chapters to follow, we show you how that may be done.

CHAPTER

2

Selecting an Appraisal System

Selection of an appraisal system can be likened to the selection of a computer system. No one in his or her right mind would call a computer company and say, "Send me a computer" without specifying how the computer would be used. The "performance appraisal store" carries a number of models varying in scope and complexity. As with the selection of a computer, the selection of an appraisal system requires the user to specify how the system will be used in the organization. In this section of the book we will be discussing some of the potential goals and uses of an appraisal system. We will then go on a guided tour of the performance appraisal store, studying each of the models with an eye to their strengths and limitations in terms of the potential goals for an appraisal system.

GOALS OF PERFORMANCE APPRAISAL

Asking us which appraisal system is the best one for you is very much like asking a used-car salesperson which car you should buy—you might end up with a limousine when all you really needed was basic transportation. The decision about which form of appraisal is best for your organization depends on what your organization is trying to accomplish with its performance appraisal system. There are three major reasons for appraising employee performance: (1) To benefit the individual employee and his/her boss, (2) To make comparisons across employees, and (3) To make comparisons across units.

Individual Employee and Boss

The core of an effective appraisal system lies in the communication between the boss and the employee. This dialogue has a number of benefits, any of which may be the principal goal of the evaluation process. The intent of the system may be to allow (or force) the boss to meet with each of his or her employees and discuss their performance with them. In some organizations this is the only reason for having an evaluation system—and it is a very important one, especially in organizations where little dialogue will occur otherwise. Their dialogue may or may not result in any documentation. Even when there is no documentation, its value still stands since their dialogue provides a context within which coaching or counseling can take place on a formal, organized basis.

Perhaps the intent of the appraisal system is to have each employee consider his or her performance, career objectives, and organizational needs and opportunities and then to create, with all of this information in mind, an employee development plan for the subsequent review period.

The appraisal system may be designed to allow each boss and subordinate to develop performance objectives (á la management by objectives) and to meet on a regular basis to discuss progress and problems in achieving objectives.

If the organization's reasons for adopting a performance appraisal system fall within this category, a simple essay appraisal system can serve the purpose well.

The focus of the boss-employee dialogue is feedback to the employee about his performance. As we consider the reasons for appraisal, we should also consider the requisites for effective feedback. To have an impact, feedback should be:

- as close in time as possible to actual job performance;
- specific rather than general (Telling an employee that he is not "pulling his weight" in the department is a far cry from telling the person that "three out of the last four times that Saturday morning work was required, you refused to help.")
- focussed on the important aspects of the job;
- related to a performance objective or standard;
- focussed on aspects of performance that the employee can do something about;
- addressing issues of performance and behavior, rather than attempting to delve into the psychological makeup of the employee.

Comparisons between Employees

The purpose of appraising employee performance may go beyond employee-boss communication. The organization may have a need to make comparisons between and across individuals throughout its levels. Perhaps the annual salary adjustments are directly related to an individual's performance. Or the promotional system may rely on input from the evaluation system. Or disciplinary actions may consider past performance. If the organization intends to rely on its appraisal system to provide information for these sorts of uses, then the appraisal system must provide data in forms suitable for making valid comparisons. This means that the appraisal must include a numerical score.

Comparisons between Departments/Units/Groups

Some organizations combine the results of individual performance appraisals to provide information on the performance of a larger unit—a division, department, or other group. An organization may want to study performance at this macro level in order to:

- provide feedback to unit managers on the relative standing of their unit;
- provide input to top management for determining which departments will receive more, or less, of the total compensation pie;
- identify "easy" and "hard" raters (See Chapter 4 on rater errors);
- furnish data for Equal Employment Opportunity (EEO) analysis

For example, one organization with which we are familiar uses performance appraisal results to determine departmental ranking, to identify rater errors, and for EEO analysis. Tables 2.1, 2.2, and 2.3 present performance data grouped for such analyses.

It goes without saying that analyses such as those presented in Tables 2.1, 2.2, and 2.3 require the inclusion of numerical data in the appraisal system. The same can be said for any other comparisons across departments or units—it is impossible to use essay-type appraisals for making meaningful comparisons among those appraised. Imagine how difficult it would be to rank fifty employees from "best" to "worst" on the basis of an essay appraisal; and, if fifty is a difficult task, what would happen in a large organization with twenty departments and fifteen hundred employees? A task of no mean dimensions to be sure! Moreover, it should be mentioned that when reading essay appraisals, one often has the feeling that one is learning more about the writing skill of the evaluator than about the performance of the person being evaluated.

Study Table 2.1 for a few minutes. What questions are generated by the summarized results? Two observations emerge immediately. First of all, Department C. employees received the highest average rating on 19 out of 20 criteria. This suggests one of two possibilities: either the employees in Department C. are the best employees, or the raters in Department C. have given inflated ratings. The data can't give the answer, but it surely raises the question. Similarly, the employees of Department E. received the lowest average ratings on 10 out of the 20 criteria. Again, this fact raises a question: are the employees of Department E. performing at that low level or are the raters of Department E. overly harsh in their ratings?

Table 2.1. Average rating by department for each criterion

Department

Criteria	A	B	C	D	E	F
1	3.63	3.54	4.66	4.00	2.70	3.09
2	3.71	3.86	4.33	3.38	3.05	2.78
3	3.67	4.05	4.50	3.53	2.41	3.38
4	3.98	3.55	4.83	3.61	2.31	2.62
5	3.80	3.33	4.50	3.53	2.73	2.61
6	3.95	3.29	4.16	2.92	3.00	2.83
7	4.07	3.17	4.66	2.92	2.86	2.76
8	3.49	2.35	4.16	3.00	2.81	2.54
9	3.86	3.50	4.66	3.84	2.12	2.80
10	3.72	3.07	4.00	3.38	2.62	3.19
11	3.69	2.76	4.33	3.61	2.50	2.51
12	3.55	2.77	4.50	3.07	2.37	2.63
13	4.38	3.78	4.16	4.27	3.76	3.33
14	3.55	3.12	4.20	3.69	2.37	3.65
15	4.14	3.97	4.16	3.46	3.43	3.31
16	3.09	2.64	4.16	3.00	2.56	2.69
17	2.87	2.85	4.16	3.15	2.60	2.10
18	3.50	3.25	4.66	3.69	2.85	2.66
19	2.91	2.76	4.16	3.38	2.35	2.64
20	2.87	2.35	4.50	2.66	2.81	1.70

Rating scale: 5 = Outstanding
4 = Exceeds expectations
3 = Meets expectations
2 = Needs improvement
1 = Unsatisfactory

Table 2.2. Average ratings given by raters at different organizational levels

Organizational level

Criteria	Top mgmt	Mid mgmt	First level	Staff
1	3.80	3.68	3.53	3.82
2	3.97	4.03	3.74	3.35
3	3.80	4.09	3.92	4.12
4	3.97	4.02	3.88	3.65
5	3.76	3.54	3.40	4.08
6	3.91	4.25	4.11	4.11
7	4.14	3.95	3.72	3.93
8	3.56	3.36	3.16	3.40
9	3.84	3.71	3.42	3.73
10	3.72	3.45	3.33	3.14
11	3.55	3.39	3.33	3.26
12	3.50	3.31	2.79	3.19
13	4.47	4.34	4.26	4.35
14	3.55	3.97	3.64	3.68
15	4.26	3.93	3.98	3.86
16	3.19	3.23	3.21	2.55
17	3.14	3.18	3.16	2.69
18	3.61	3.54	3.47	3.54
19	3.29	3.54	3.46	2.36
20	2.95	3.33	2.91	2.39

Rating scale: 5 = Outstanding
4 = Exceeds expectations
3 = Meets expectations
2 = Needs improvement
1 = Unsatisfactory

Table 2.3. Average rating received by different groups

Race

Criteria	1 White	2 Black	3 Asian	4 Other
1	3.70	3.40	3.00	4.22
2	3.27	3.50	4.00	3.45
3	3.56	3.80	4.30	4.36
4	3.73	4.00	4.00	3.71
5	4.28	2.75	3.00	4.00
6	4.27	3.40	4.50	4.00
7	4.19	3.00	3.00	3.57
8	3.67	2.00	3.33	3.44
9	2.48	3.80	3.04	2.76
10	3.25	3.75	3.62	3.44
11	3.48	3.16	3.08	2.42
12	3.27	2.00	2.10	3.36
13	4.57	2.50	3.00	3.67
14	3.80	4.00	3.60	3.72
15	3.89	3.75	4.04	3.72
16	3.69	2.50	4.00	3.77
17	2.86	3.66	4.60	2.50
18	3.31	3.90	3.30	3.88
19	2.00	4.20	3.00	3.50
20	4.25	4.00	4.10	4.55

Rating scale: 5 = Outstanding
4 = Exceeds expectations
3 = Meets expectations
2 = Needs improvement
1 = Unsatisfactory

Study the summary data presented in Table 2.2. What does the data suggest? Two conclusions are immediately suggested: the "easiest" raters appear to be top management, followed closely by mid-management. The "harshest" raters seem to be the first-level supervisors. Are these conclusions fair? They may or may not be. For example, if a number of hourly employees were recently hired, then the low ratings given by first-line supervisors may be very accurate. Another "if," if the organization has a superior program for identifying and promoting employees with management potential, then the "high" ratings given by top- and mid-level managers might indeed be accurate. Again, the data raises the questions but can't give the answers.

Study the summary data presented in Table 2.3. Can you draw any conclusions? There appear to be no systematic differences in the ratings based on the race of the person being evaluated. Race does not seem to have a bearing on the evaluation results.

SOME TECHNICAL CONSIDERATIONS

During the design stage we should pay close attention not only to the goals of our appraisal system, but also to the technical quality of the system. The major technical criteria are: reliability, validity, time and cost involved in development and use, and usefulness to rater and ratee. We will discuss these criteria individually.

Reliability

How reliable will the system be? Reliability is a matter of reproducibility and consistency. Will the appraisal results be reproducible—that is, if a person's performance remains for all practical purposes unchanged, will he or she receive an appraisal that is very similar at the next review? Will the raters in your organization use the system in essentially the same fashion? If different raters (more than one superior, peers, subordinates, self, clients, customers, etc.) participate in the appraisal of one employee, will there be more agreement than disagreement in the ratings given? If two different raters are rating two different employees whose performance is generally acknowledged to be the same, will the ratings the employees receive be highly similar?

While discussions of reliability often have a theoretical tone, research on reliability does have practical implications for appraisal systems. The following factors have all been shown to have an impact on reliability:

1. Number of criteria—Reliability increases as the number of criteria increase. Appraisal systems that include at least ten and no more than twenty-five criteria tend to have higher reliabilities.
2. The scale itself—Scales that are balanced, such as Scale A. in Table 2.4 encourage the rater to use a wider range of scale values, thereby increasing reliability. Lopsided scales, such as Scale B., can actually

reduce reliability. Also, the number of scale values should be large enough to allow a good range of ratings, e.g., four scale values as in Scale C. However, more than nine scale values adds little to the rating process. In our work we have found that five scale values, as in Scale A., works quite well.

A word on semantics—don't use "average." Many employees, raters and ratees alike, consider a rating of "average" to be less-than-satisfactory.

Table 2.4. Sample rating scales.

Scale A.
5. Outstanding
4. Exceeds expectations
3. Meets expectations
2. Needs improvement
1. Unsatisfactory

Scale B.
5. Excellent
4. Outstanding
3. Superior
2. Full performance
1. Unacceptable

Scale C.
4. Exceeds expectations
3. Meets expectations
2. Below standard
1. Unsatisfactory

Case 2.1

One organization used multiple ratings (by different raters) for each employee. These multiple ratings included appraisal by two levels of supervision, peer evaluations, subordinate evaluations, and self-evaluation. Statistical analysis of all ratings were conducted. For each person rated the following information was correlated: average superior rating, average peer rating, average subordinate rating, and self rating. All intercorrelations between these four sets of data were computed. The average intercorrelation was close to $r = .50$, indicating that there was a significant degree of consistency across the different rating groups.

Validity

The validity of an appraisal system is a matter of its job-relatedness, the question of whether the performance appraisal system accurately assesses and reflects a person's true performance. Are the rating criteria germane to the job? Are the rating criteria appropriate, e.g., specific, for the job being appraised?

For example, quality and quantity of work, while important concepts, are far too general unless there is further elaboration about what is meant by quality and quantity. Decision making ability or ability to program a word processing machine are both much more specific. Are the standards of performance for each criterion spelled out? Do the performance standards apply to the job? Will the evaluation system yield specific information about an individual's performance?

The notion of validity implies that there will be different criteria used to evaluate performance in different jobs. When we say different criteria for different jobs, we are suggesting that you go well beyond any gross differences like salaried versus hourly or exempt versus non-exempt. Research indicates that jobs can be grouped into meaningful clusters for purposes of formulating criteria. Some of these clusters might be:

- upper managerial jobs
- mid-management
- first-level management
- secretarial-clerical
- research jobs
- police officer
- custodial jobs
- food service jobs
- nursing jobs

Before leaving the topic of validity, the relationship between reliability and validity must be addressed. An appraisal instrument must be reliable before it can be valid. However, reliability does not guarantee validity. For example, an appraisal instrument that was carefully designed for assessing performance in a custodial job and was subsequently used to assess the performance of food service employees would be reliable but not valid for the food service employee job.

Time and Cost of Development

Evaluation systems cover the gamut from "quick-and-dirty" to systematic approaches that focus on various clusters of jobs (often referred to as job families) throughout the organization. There are radical differences in the amount of time and money required to develop different systems. For example, an essay evaluation form requires only a few hours of developmental effort. A behaviorally anchored approach (where both the criteria and standards are defined), on the other hand, can easily take three to six months of developmental effort.

Time and Cost of Use

The appraisal process itself comes in a wide variety of shapes and sizes. Some systems require little monitoring, demand a minimum of time for completion of forms, and are onerous for only those managers who appraise really large numbers of employees (fifteen to twenty employees or more). Other approaches to appraisal require attention from the rater throughout the year and significant amounts of time for the appraisal process itself.

Acceptance by Users

Last, but by no means least, is the matter of acceptance by employees. A particular appraisal system may be reliable, valid, and require what is seen as a reasonable amount of time and cost to develop, and yet be undesirable from the point of view of those who will have to use it. From the rater's perspective, how easy or how difficult will the system be to use? How much time will be required to complete the form? How long is the form? What documentation must be kept during the rating period? What do raters perceive to be the relative costs and benefits of the evaluation system?

From the ratee's perspective, does the appraisal system provide for a meaningful evaluation? Are performance goals or job standards an integral part of the system? Does the feedback promise to be meaningful and useful? Is there space for comments? Does the system include a planning and development component? Do ratees view the system as something positive or as a waste of time?

The appraisal system must also be considered in the context of the organization. The performance appraisal system will not exist in a vacuum. On the contrary, it will be housed in a specific organization which has a specific history. We must be sure to ask: What has been the organization's experience with performance appraisal systems? Have the experiences been positive, neutral, or negative? What have people liked/disliked about previous evaluation systems? Past experience can supply pertinent information for use in choosing present and future strategies.

Up to this point in the chapter the focus has been on a number of ideas surrounding the appraisal system. We stressed the importance of articulating the goals of your appraisal system, and we discussed eight technical considerations (Usefulness in providing feedback to the employee, numerical ratings for administrative purposes, reliability, validity, time/cost of development, time/cost of use, rater acceptance, and ratee acceptance) that can influence your choice of an appraisal system. We are now ready to turn our attention to the various methods of appraisal.

COMMON EVALUATION SYSTEMS

As in other management decisions, the selection of an appraisal system involves many trade-offs. In this section we will be presenting the following major approaches to appraisal:

- essay
- ranking
- management by objectives/results/accountabilities

- criteria only
- criteria and standards

Not only will we provide descriptions and examples of these appraisal systems, we will also critique each system using the technical, personal, and organizational considerations discussed earlier. Each of these systems has something substantial to offer, and each has its own drawbacks.

The Essay Approach

As its name suggests, the essay approach to appraisal requires the rater to respond to one or more open-ended essay-type questions concerning the performance of the person being rated. The typical essay appraisal includes five or six questions and is two or three pages in length. Figure 2.1 presents an essay appraisal form. (All of the appraisal forms presented in this chapter have been or are currently being used in organizations.) Another example of an essay appraisal is presented in Appendix B.

If we evaluate the essay approach using the eight factors mentioned earlier, we will find that:

1. Usefulness in providing feedback to the employee—It may or it may not be useful depending on the amount of detail provided by the rater. The quality of the feedback is totally dependent on the rater.
2. Numerical rating for administrative purposes—Not possible with an essay. There is no satisfactory method of assigning numerical values to essays.
3. Reliability—It is quite difficult to assess the reliability of essay appraisals. However, attempts to assign numerical values to essay appraisals suggest that essay appraisals are not reliable. This is due, in large part, to the highly subjective nature of essay appraisals. The reliability of essay appraisals increases as the content of the appraisal becomes more objective.
4. Validity—Essays are valid to the extent that they focus on job-related criteria. However, the validity of the essay is difficult to establish for the same reasons that reliability is difficult to establish.
5. Time/cost of development—The essay is very easy to develop.
6. Time/cost of use—The essay, properly done, takes a lot of time.
7. Rater acceptance—May be high or low, depending on the rater.
8. Ratee acceptance—May be high or low, depending on the quality of the feedback provided.

EMPLOYEE PERFORMANCE APPRAISAL

NAME OF EMPLOYEE		OFFICE	
SOCIAL SECURITY NUMBER	JOB TITLE	SECTION	
TIME PERIOD COVERED	TYPE OF APPRAISAL ANNUAL ☐ SPECIAL ☐	DATE OF REVIEW	

I. APPRAISAL OF PERFORMANCE:
   A. WAS THE REGULAR DAY TO DAY WORK DONE AS EXPECTED?
      YES ☐   NO ☐   PARTIALLY ☐

   B. WERE THE MAJOR RESULTS REQUIRED OF THIS POSITION ACHIEVED?
      YES ☐   NO ☐   PARTIALLY ☐

   C. TO WHAT EXTENT AND HOW WELL WERE THEY ACHIEVED?

   D. IF THERE WERE PROBLEMS WHAT ACTIONS WERE TAKEN?

   E. WHAT IMPROVEMENT IS NEEDED IN THIS AREA?

II. APPRAISAL OF WORKING RELATIONSHIPS:
   A. HOW WELL DID THE EMPLOYEE ESTABLISH AND MAINTAIN RELATIONSHIPS WITH OTHER PEOPLE THAT WERE NECESSARY TO GETTING RESULTS IN THIS JOB?

   B. IF THERE WERE PROBLEMS WHAT ACTION WAS TAKEN?

   C. WHAT IMPROVEMENT IS NEEDED IN THIS AREA?

III. EMPLOYEE DEVELOPMENT:
   A. LIST DEVELOPMENTAL OPPORTUNITIES PLANNED WITH THIS EMPLOYEE
      1. FOR IMPROVEMENT ON PRESENT JOB:

Figure 2.1. Sample of an essay appraisal form.

III. EMPLOYEE DEVELOPMENT (CONT'D)
   A. LIST DEVELOPMENTAL OPPORTUNITIES PLANNED WITH THIS EMPLOYEE:
      2. FOR ADVANCEMENT:

IV. SUMMARY APPRAISAL:

V. EMPLOYEE COMMENTS:
   A. WHAT STEPS CAN YOU TAKE TO IMPROVE YOUR PERFORMANCE?

   B. WHAT ASSISTANCE DO YOU NEED FROM YOUR SUPERVISOR TO IMPROVE YOUR PERFORMANCE?

   C. WHAT ADDITIONAL TRAINING WILL ASSIST YOU IN IMPROVING YOUR JOB PERFORMANCE?

Figure 2.1. Continued

Ranking

The ranking approach to appraisal requires the rater to "line-up" his or her employees from best to worst. Ranking is used most frequently in conjunction with salary decisions to determine how much of a merit (performance-based) increase each employee will receive. Ranking may be a very straightforward process such as the following: "Rank your employees in terms of their overall performance during the last year, starting with your best employee and ending with the employee you would rate last. You may not have any ties."

Employees might be ranked according to one global criterion, such as overall performance, or according to a number of different criteria, such as quality of work, leadership ability, coordination skills, etc.; these more specific rankings would then be averaged in order to arrive at an overall ranking. A sample of a ranking appraisal format is presented in Figure 2.2.

Instructions

Please read these instructions all the way through before ranking anyone.

There are _____ Unipolar Alternation Ranking Forms following these instructions. You are to complete each form before going on to the next form, and you are to fill them out in the order in which they are presented. All of the directions below apply to each form.

1. Write your name on the top of the rating form.
2. Read the list of names on the left hand side of the ranking form.
3. Look over the list of names and decide which one individual is *best* described by the rating characteristic. Draw a line through that individual's name and number and write both the name and number in the blank space on the right side of the words "1 most descriptive of."
4. Look over the remaining names and decide which one individual is *least* well described by the rating characteristic. Draw a line through the individual's name and number and write both the name and number in the blank space on the right side of the words "2 least descriptive of."
5. Next out of those names remaining on your list, select the individual you think is *best* described by the rating characteristic. As before draw a line through his name and number and write both the name and number in the blank space on the right side of the words "3 next most descriptive of."
6. Next out of the names remaining on your list, select the individual who is *least* well described by the rating characteristic. As before, draw a line through this individual's name and number, and write down the name and number in the blank space to the right of the words "4 next least descriptive of."
7. Continue this ranking procedure (selecting the individual for whom the rating characteristic is most descriptive and then the one for whom the rating characteristic is least descriptive) until you have drawn a line through each name and number on the list.

Figure 2.2. Example of a ranking appraisal form.

RANKING FORM

Your Name: _____ Department: _____ Date: _____

Rating characteristic: Effective written communications

Definition: This rating factor involves composition of reports, directives, letters, memos, proposals, and other documents and the use of good principles of writing such as clarity, brevity, appropriate format, sufficient documentation, etc.

Individuals to be ranked Note: Cross off each name after you rank it.		ranking order	Individuals whom you have ranked		
Individual names	number		The above rating characteristic is	Individual's name	number
Martin Rand	2078	1	most descriptive of		
Mary Bennett	2079	3	next most descriptive of		
Joe Bjordal	2081	5	next most descriptive of		
Howard Nichols	2083	7	next most descriptive of		
Jerry O'Brien	2089	9	next most descriptive of		
David Nakamoto	2091	11	next most descriptive of		
Charlene Neves	2092	13	next most descriptive of		
Robert Telson	2093	15	next most descriptive of		
Harry Turner	2095	17	next most descriptive of		
Sylvia Vasks	2099	19	next most descriptive of		
Shirley Rice	3002	20	next least descriptive of		
Helen Rodriguez	3003	18	next least descriptive of		
		16	next least descriptive of		
		14	next least descriptive of		
		12	next least descriptive of		
		10	next least descriptive of		
		8	next least descriptive of		
		6	next least descriptive of		
		4	next least descriptive of		
		2	least descriptive of		

Figure 2.2. Continued

An analysis of the ranking approach yields the following conclusions:

1. Usefulness in providing feedback to the employee—The result of a ranking provides little meaningful feedback. It might be nice to know that you're ranked number one, but left unanswered are the questions of what you did, or didn't do, to deserve that rank.
2. Numerical rating for administrative purposes—Ranking does result in a numerical rating. However, ranking results in an ordinal type scale, much like the results of (to make an unflattering comparison) a horse race. Ranking tells us nothing about the relative difference between the ranks. One and two might be very close, with a large gap between two and three.
3. Reliability—Ranking is a more reliable form of appraisal than the essay, but it still leaves much to be desired. Often the only reliable ranks are the very first and the very last. Those ranked in the middle tend to shift ranks as re-ranking occurs, even when the re-ranking is done only a day or two later.
4. Validity—When the ranking criteria are job-related, then one might argue that the ranking is valid. However, validity cannot be present without a reliable evaluation system; therefore the validity of the ranking approach to appraisal is dubious at best.
5. Time/cost of development—The ranking criteria and forms can be developed with only a few hours of work.
6. Time/cost of use—Ranking is fairly easy for the rater to accomplish. Of all the evaluation techniques, ranking requires the least amount of time to use.
7. Rater acceptance—If the rankings are not shared with the employees, as is often the case when this approach to appraisal is used, raters usually will have minimal resistance. The main complaint voiced with a ranking approach to appraisal is that there is no fair way to compare ranks across different departments. The #2 rank in Department X may not be as good as the #5 rank in Department Y which happens to be staffed with a truly outstanding group of employees. If the rankings must be shared with the employees, then there will be significant rater resistance since rankings are very difficult to explain (defend?) to the satisfaction of the employee being ranked.
8. Ratee acceptance—Employees, for the most part, do not like ranking approaches; the approach is viewed as out of their personal control, and the feedback they receive is minimal.

Management by Objectives/Results/Accountabilities

Most managers have been exposed to some version of management by objectives (MBO). "Management by objectives" is a relatively broad term encompassing all approaches that include two major elements: (1) at some point in the appraisal process—preferably at the onset—superior and subordinate meet to discuss goals and to jointly establish goals for the subordinate; and (2) the superior and subordinate subsequently meet to appraise the subordinate's performance in terms of the pre-established goals. Ideally, objectives for an individual employee evolve, at least in part, from the total organization objectives as represented by departmental or unit objectives.

Figure 2.3 presents a typical "management by objectives" performance appraisal format.

Evaluating the management by objectives approach we can draw the following conclusions:

1. Usefulness in providing feedback to the employee—If the objectives include specific performance standards (as is the case in Figure 2.3.), there is potential for a high degree of feedback regarding those objectives. However, since many management by objectives approaches recommend developing only five or six objectives, there may be important aspects of the job for which no objectives/standards are specified, and consequently no feedback given.

2. Numerical rating for administrative purposes—It is difficult to assign numerical ratings to objectives since there is often no valid basis for comparison across objectives for different employees, even employees performing the same job. Similarly, it is nearly impossible to compare different objectives in terms of their level of difficulty. The resulting dilemma is that establishing quantitative standards for different jobs in terms of the particular objectives may be impossible: Phillip may have four easy objectives and accomplish all of them, while Michelle may have four difficult objectives and accomplish only two of them. In reality, Michelle's performance far exceeds Phillip's; but since Michelle and Phillip work in different departments performing different jobs for different bosses, there is no means of determining the relative difficulty, complexity, etc. of their objectives.

3. Reliability—If performance standards are developed for each objective (as in Figure 2.3.), there is a potential for a high degree of reliability. Without the supporting standards, reliability will probably be low.

4. Validity—If the objectives are central to the major responsibilities and accountabilities of the job, then they will be job-related and, therefore, valid. Without specific standards for each objective, however, one may question whether rating performance against a particular objective actually reflects the ratee's level of performance.

PRINCIPLE ACCOUNTABILITIES	SPECIFIC OBJECTIVES	STANDARDS	TARGET DATES	
List in order of importance, the key accountabilities of your job—those specific areas within which you are held accountable for producing results.	For each accountability, state specifically the end results you plan to accomplish during the time period covered.	For each Specific Objective, list the measures such as cost or quality indicators that must be considered in accomplishing the objective. Indicate when the objective must be achieved, i.e., weekly, monthly or a specific date.	Planned	Actual

SIGNATURES

Employee _____ Date _____

Supervisor _____ Date _____

Reviewed by: _____ Date _____

Figure 2.3. Example of a management by objectives appraisal form.

PERFORMANCE REVIEWS							
6 MONTHS based on completion of objectives to date				**1 YEAR** based on achievement of entire objective			
ACHIEVEMENT LEVEL			COMMENTS FOR REVIEW	ACHIEVEMENT LEVEL			COMMENTS FOR REVIEW
Exceeded	Achieved	Partially met	Little or no action	Exceeded	Achieved	Partially met	Little or no action
			Use this column to support the achievement level indicated. If revisions are made on the original objectives and standards, state the reason and adjustment here.				Use this column to support the achievement level indicated. If revisions are made on the original objectives and standards, state the reason and adjustment here.

UNPLANNED ACCCOMPLISHMENTS

List other accomplishments achieved by this employee not listed above.

Figure 2.3. Continued

5. Time/cost of development—A management by objectives system requires very little time to design since there are so many models available.
6. Time/cost of use—The process of developing objectives and standards can easily require five to ten hours per employee.
7. Rater acceptance—If raters are required to develop both objectives and standards for each objective, the significant amount of time required often inspires at least some resistance. The results of the performance appraisal based on the objectives and standards are often intended for use in making salary decisions. If this is the case, raters may find that it is extremely difficult to make the transition from appraisal to salary action because of the difficulty (mentioned above) in quantifying objectives.
8. Ratee acceptance—Employees usually will like the management by objective approach if (and this is a significant "if") they are truly involved in the development of both the objectives and the standards.

Case 2.2

The XYZ corporation had a policy of rotating supervisors to a new position every three months. There were four major jobs through which the supervisors would rotate. Supervisors had the option of bidding for a particular job, which would be awarded or refused on the basis of seniority and experience. One week before the rotation, the department manager informed each supervisor of his or her next assignment.

After making the assignments for the spring rotation, the manager gave each of the supervisors a sealed envelope. Each envelope contained a carefully thought out and well developed statement of the objectives and standards for the supervisor's next job. The manager had spent from fifteen to twenty hours on each of the four jobs developing the objectives and standards. From a technical point of view, the objectives and standards were of the highest quality. However, the supervisors were extremely upset over two things: (1) the impersonal way in which they were given the objectives and standards, and (2) the fact that they had no involvement at all in developing the objectives and standards. The technical excellence of the objectives could not compensate for the inattention to human needs and interests.

Criteria only

In the criteria-only approach to appraisal, rating criteria (sometimes referred to as rating factors) are listed without accompanying performance standards for each criterion, hence the title criteria-only. The rating criteria include "hard" criteria (cost control, return on investment), traits (initiative, creativity), and "soft" criteria (interpersonal skills, decision making skills). The list is accompanied by a generalized rating scale giving defintions for various levels of performance (See Figure 2.4.); however, the definitions are not specific to each criterion. This is analogous to the management by objectives approach when objectives are unaccompanied by specific performance standards.

This section evaluates the skills, knowledge, and techniques an employee applies in achieving the desired job objective. Using the standards indicated below, rate the employee's performance in the evaluation.

STANDARDS FOR REVIEW

CODE

1. Distinguished: Clearly outstanding—Performance far exceeds the job's requirements in all respects—Only the best belong at this level.

2. Commendable: Above acceptable—Performance is noticeably better than required by the job. Long seasoned and highly proficient employees belong here.

3. Competent: Satisfactory—Performance meets the job's requirements, overall. This is the level of performance expected of most seasoned employees. It implies that the employee achieved all that is expected of the position. A majority of employees belong at this level.

4. Provisional: Improvement needed—Performance falls short of meeting the job's requirements in one or more significant areas. This is normally reserved for inexperienced new incumbents and others who are performing at less than the job's expectations. At this level, there is a demonstrable need for improvement.

A. Work Management Skills

Regardless of whether an employee is in a management position, responsible for securing results through the efforts of others, or is in a professional/technical position and is responsible primarily for his or her own results, there are basic work management skills that must be applied in achieving job objectives. Consider the abilities the employee has demonstrated in the following areas.

Planning

— Forecasts and anticipates future conditions and events that will affect work objectives.
— Sets or recommends realistic, measurable, results-oriented objectives.
— Establishes and sequences logical action steps and time schedules for achievement of objectives.
— Determines accurately the necessary manpower, equipment, and financial resources to achieve objectives.
— Analyzes the cost of achieving an objective in relation to the return its accomplishment will bring before making recommendations.
— As required, formulates clear and concise policies and procedures for achievement of objectives.

Comments:

RATING
1 2 3 4

Figure 2.4. Example of a criteria-only appraisal form.

	RATING
Organization —Arranges and relates work assignments so that objectives are accomplished effectively, involving the fewest people necessary at the least cost. —Eliminates or minimizes overlap and duplication of effort. —Effectively utilizes time available. —Understands and works within limits of designated authority and responsibility. —Delegates work as appropriate. —Demonstrates understanding of line/staff relationships and responsibilities in working with superiors, peers, and subordinates. **Comments:**	1 2 3 4
Leadership —Makes decisions based on rational analysis of related factors and consequences rather than spontaneous reaction. —Creates understanding and acceptance in both oral and written communications. —Contributes to team efforts and is effective in motivating others to work toward accomplishment of common objectives. —As required, selects qualified people to perform the work to be done. —As required, works with subordinates to improve knowledge, skills, and attributes required to achieve objectives. **Comments:**	1 2 3 4
Controlling —Develops and/or utilizes specific criteria or standards through which results can be measured. —Records and reports work being done and results accomplished. —Analyzes and evaluates the quality of the work done and the results secured in relation to the standard set. —Takes corrective action to meet specified standards and secure the results desired. **Comments:**	1 2 3 4

Figure 2.4. Continued

B. Technical Skills and Knowledge	RATING
Describe below the specific technical skills and knowledge required to perform this position. Evaluate the degree of proficiency the employee demonstrates in applying these to the job objectives.	
Skill:	1　2　3　4
Skill:	1　2　3　4
Skill:	1　2　3　4
Skill:	1　2　3　4
Comments:	

C. Additional Performance Criteria

List here and comment on any other factors you believe to be relevant in evaluating this employee's performance.

Figure 2.4. Continued

Many of the performance appraisal systems currently operating fit into the "criteria-only" category. In the more sophisticated criteria-only systems, different sets of criteria are developed for different families of jobs. Figure 2.4. presents a criteria-only approach developed for a group of managers in one organization.

Applying the eight factors to evaluate the criteria-only approach:

1. Usefulness in providing feedback to the employee—Once again, to the extent that the criteria are job-related, the feedback should prove useful. However, since the performance standards are not specific to a particular criterion, the feedback tends to be too vague or generalized to be useful. In addition the performance standard definitions do not tell the employee what he must do in order to achieve a particular performance rating.
2. Numerical rating for administrative purposes—A numerical rating is an integral part of the approach to appraisal and is one of its advantages. However, the numerical rating leaves something to be desired. Comments under "validity" elaborate on this point.
3. Reliability—A numerical rating system has the potential of high reliability only if the ratings are based on specific performance standards. Since criteria-only systems lack performance standards, their reliability suffers.

4. Validity—Two factors must be considered. If the criteria are specific to a particular job or job family, then the appraisal is job-related. However, without any definition of performance standards for each of the criteria, the degree to which a performance rating actually represents a particular level of performance may vary from rater to rater. The validity of job-specific criteria-only appraisal techniques is acceptable.
5. Time/cost of development—The criteria for a particular job family can easily be developed by a group of four or five employees in a half-day or less.
6. Time/cost of use—The amount of time required to use this system depends on the amount of justification (comments to support the ratings) required by the system designers. The greater the degree of justification required, the higher the cost of use. If no justification is required, the criteria-only approach is very easy to use.
7. Rater acceptance—This approach to evaluation is usually viewed as a relatively easy and straightforward one from the rater's perspective.
8. Ratee acceptance—If justifications for the ratings are included in the system, ratee acceptance is high. However, most criteria-only approaches do not require justifications (they are optional); therefore ratee acceptance tends to be moderate.

Criteria and Standards

The criteria and standards approach to evaluation goes one step beyond the criteria-only approach: performance standards are developed for each of the criteria. The process involves three steps:

Step One—Identify groups of similar jobs (job families).

Step Two—Develop performance criteria.

Step Three—Develop standards of performance for each of the criteria.

The number of performance standards depends on the number of rating points in your rating scale. If you want to have a three point scale, e.g., 1 = unsatisfactory, 2 = satisfactory, 3 = exceeds expectations, then you should develop standards for each of the three points on your scale. The standards answer the questions of "How good is good" or "How bad is bad?" Notice that we are developing standards for *each* of the criteria. For instance, satisfactory performance for planning ability is defined differently from satisfactory performance for employee counseling ability. Figure 2.5. presents examples of two criteria that include performance standards. Additional examples are presented in the Appendix.

CRITERION ONE—PLANNING

This aspect of the job involves designing, scheduling, and implementing short and long range plans; scheduling workload within plan; anticipating deviations from the plan.

These statements describe persons who are usually rated *outstanding* on planning by most raters.

5. _____ Develops several clear alternative action plans to achieve objectives
   _____ Initiates alternative plans when original objectives are not being met.
   _____ Questions current plans against lost or developing opportunities

These statements describe persons who are usually rated *exceeding job standards* on planning by most raters.

4. _____ Anticipates arising problems with prepared contingency plans
   _____ Keeps goals and objectives clearly and frequently in front of subordinates
   _____ Meets with those concerned to review the work situation, asking for inputs in developing problems/opportunities

These statements describe persons who are usually rated *meeting job standards* on planning by most raters.

3. _____ Reviews action plans with superior
   _____ Has plan objectives which fit the needs of other departments
   _____ Completes status reports on time
   _____ Maintains planning process without attempting to improve it
   _____ Has "stretch" in plan but does not indicate how it will be done

These statements describe persons who are usually rated as *needing improvement* on planning by most raters.

2. _____ Completes plan late
   _____ Holds planning meetings only when requested by superior or peers
   _____ Plans do not contain alternatives

These statements describe persons who are usually rated *unsatisfactory* in planning by most raters.

1. _____ Plans only when forced to plan by superior
   _____ Does not involve subordinates in the planning process
   _____ Plans do not include objectives
   _____ Plans contain unrealistic assumptions

0. _____ This criterion is not applicable or I have not had the opportunity to observe performance on this criterion.

Figure 2.5. Example of a criteria and standards appraisal form.

CRITERION TWO—ACCEPTING RESPONSIBILITY AND INITIATING ACTION

This aspect of the job involves the amount of personal responsibility taken for the completion of work, the amount of work progress made without complete supervisory direction, the willingness to think through work barriers and to keep working toward priority goals, to follow up on work that seems necessary to achieve priority job or unit goals.

These statements describe persons who are usually rated *outstanding* on accepting responsibility and initiating action by most raters.	5. _____ _____ _____ _____	Anticipates problems and tries to eliminate them. Advances unit goals in ways others overlook. Assumes responsibility for making his/her job or unit the best. Stays informed on "higher level" needs.
These statements describe persons who are usually rated as *exceeding job standards* on accepting responsibility and initiating action by most raters.	4. _____ _____ _____ _____	Not afraid of making mistakes and accepting the blame. Accepts additional responsibility. Takes action on problems even when supervisor out. Conceives and carries through jobs on own initiative.
These statements describe persons who are usually rated as *meeting job standards* on accepting responsibility and initiating action by most raters.	3. _____ _____	Takes action on all tasks which are due to be completed. Completes job even without specific instructions.
These statements describe persons who are usually rated *below job standards* on accepting responsibility and initiating action by most raters.	2. _____ _____ _____ _____	Doesn't want to do work. Takes "own time" to get work done. Neglects the work s/he is not interested in. Won't initiate action on own.
These statements describe persons who are usually rated as *unacceptable* on accepting responsibility and initiating action by most raters.	1. _____ _____ _____ _____	Fills time by doing personal things. Completes task only under direct supervision. Requires 100% guidance to get things done. Cannot be left to work without supervision.
	0. _____	This criterion is not applicable or I have not had the opportunity to observe performance on this criterion.

Figure 2.5. Continued

Applying the eight factors to the criteria and standards approach to appraisal yields the following conclusions:

1. Usefulness in providing feedback to the employee—If the criteria are job-related and if the standards are clearly defined, then the criteria and standards approach provides a high degree of specific feedback to the employee.
2. Numerical rating for administrative purposes—A numerical rating is an integral part of this approach to evaluation.
3. Reliability—Criteria and standards approaches to appraisal usually have the highest reliability. This high degree of reliability can be attributed to the performance standards which give raters a more consistent frame of reference when appraising a particular employee's performance.
4. Validity—Criteria and standards have a high degree of validity because the criteria are job related and the standards are designed to reflect different degrees of performance for each of the criteria.
5. Time/cost of development—This is the most costly method of performance appraisal to develop. It can easily require two hours, or more, to define the performance standards for *each* of the criteria.
6. Time/cost of use—This approach to appraisal requires much less time to use than all of the other approaches. Much of the time the rater would ordinarily spend in justifying his or her ratings is not required, since the standards provide the justifications.
7. Rater acceptance—Raters dislike the developmental effort required; however, they do like the final product. Once developed, the criteria and standards need only be adapted for individual cases, but the work is largely done. The developmental effort is an obstacle to rater acceptance for the first time only.
8. Ratee acceptance—Ratees like the criteria and standards approach since it provides a structure often lacking in appraisal systems. Many of the questions that go unanswered in other approaches to appraisal (such as why did I receive a particular rating or what do I have to do to get a higher rating) now become an integral part of the appraisal process.

Table 2.5 presents a schematic summary of the advantages and disadvantages of the five performance appraisal approaches that we have discussed in this section. It is important to remember that the success or failure of any appraisal system is dependent on a number of factors that comprise the organizational environment.

Table 2.5. A comparison of the advantages and disadvantages of five major approaches to appraisal.

	Essay	Ranking	MBO	Criteria only	Criteria and standards
Feedback					
Numerical rating	No	No	No	Yes	Yes
Reliability	Low	Low	Low	Moderate	High
Validity	Low	Low	Low	Moderate	High
Time/cost of development	Little	Little	Little	Moderate	High
Time/cost of use	High	Little	High	Moderate	Moderate
Rater acceptance	*	Low	*	High	High
Ratee acceptance	*	Low	*	Moderate	High

*May be high, medium, or low depending on how the procedure is implemented and used.

COMMUNICATING THE GOALS OF YOUR SYSTEM

Once you have decided on the goals your appraisal system should achieve, these goals should be communicated to all of the employees involved in the appraisal system—in most organizations, virtually every employee. Since there are so many potential uses of performance appraisal results, it is vitally important to spell out exactly what use will be made of appraisal results to eliminate as much as possible misunderstandings about why the organization is using an appraisal system. Case 2.3 presents an example of what can happen even when the appraisal goals are articulated and communicated to all employees.

Case 2.3

A large organization whose appraisal practices ranged from sophisticated appraisal systems in some departments to no appraisal at all in other departments developed a uniform system for appraisal. The intent of the system was threefold: to develop performance appraisal criteria for every employee, to communicate those criteria to each employee, and to review each employee's performance regularly, at least annually. The appraisal results were not to be used for any personnel actions. These intentions were recorded in writing and given to all employees.

Nevertheless, there was still a great deal of discussion among employees at all levels of the organization about the extent to which appraisal results would impact salary actions and whether or not this was actually a merit pay system. There was also much discussion around how the appraisal results from different raters in different departments could be used as part of the promotional process (even though evaluation results were not to be used for promotions in this organization). The sole reason for the appraisal system was to increase communication between boss and subordinate—in a word, feedback. Yet, people were not convinced until two years of personal experience with the appraisal system supported the policy statement.

Appendix A. includes an outstanding example of an orientation booklet written to familiarize employees with one organization's appraisal system.

RATING YOUR ORGANIZATION'S APPRAISAL SYSTEM

Thus far we have presented the technical aspects of appraisal systems and have applied them to five different approaches to the appraisal process. To assist you in rating your organization's appraisal system. Figure 2.6. has a series of questions which you can answer with a "YES" or "NO".

	YES	NO
1. Are the goals of your appraisal system expressed in writing?	___	___
2. Are employees oriented to and/or trained in the use of the appraisal system?	___	___
3. Are there between 10 and 25 criteria for each job or job family?	___	___
4. Is there a rating scale?	___	___
5. Are there 4 to 9 scale values in the rating scale?	___	___
6. Is the scale balanced?	___	___
7. Are the criteria job related?	___	___
8. Are the criteria specific?	___	___
9. Are the standards of performance defined for each scale value?	___	___
10. Is the system cost effective?	___	___
11. Is the system accepted by raters?	___	___
12. Is the system accepted by ratees?	___	___

Figure 2.6. Assessing your appraisal system.

CHAPTER

3

Developing Performance Criteria and Standards

A manager we know and respect has a very simple rule for the performance appraisal process: "There shouldn't be any surprises in the performance appraisal process." This suggests that, first of all, the employee being appraised should have a solid understanding of the standards used in the appraisal process and, second, the employee should be receiving feedback on performance throughout the entire review period. In this chapter we will focus our attention on the first of these two points—performance standards.

Throughout this chapter we will be using two words which need some definition—"criteria" and "standards." A criterion indicates the element, factor, task, area of responsibility, skill, or ability that the employee is evaluated on. A standard is the level of performance one must achieve within a given criterion. Some managers prefer the term "expectation" to "standard." For example, a boss and employee agree that the employee should be evaluated on planning ability. In this example, planning ability is the criterion. If the boss goes on to say that she expects all plans to be developed according to an eight-step process, the employee's adherence to that planning process is one of the standards that will be used to assess his or her performance. It is not enough to tell an employee that he will be evaluated on planning ability; we must also indicate what our standards or expectations are. The reason is simple: Different people include different things in their definition of planning as well as having different ideas regarding what comprises a satisfactory or an exceptional example of planning.

WHY PERFORMANCE CRITERIA?

Why all the fuss about criteria? Can't we assume that we know what's important in our job and that the criteria will take care of themselves? Imagine that you took out a blank sheet of paper and made a list of the specific criteria that should be included in your own performance appraisal. Table 3.1 provides a simple format that can be used to answer this question. Most managers find that it takes them anywhere from ten to thirty minutes to complete this task.

Now imagine that your boss goes through the same exercise without looking at your answers.

Table 3.1 Identifying performance criteria.

In the spaces below we would like you to record those tasks, abilities, criteria, accountabilities, etc. that should be used for appraising your performance. Include only those factors that can be measured or observed and that are related to the job. Avoid such subjective factors as attitudes or personality traits. For example, some possible factors might include:

Planning ability
Communication skills
Cooperation with coworkers

1. _____
2. _____
3. _____
4. _____
5. _____
6. _____
7. _____
8. _____
9. _____
10. _____
11. _____
12. _____
13. _____
14. _____
15. _____
16. _____
17. _____
18. _____
19. _____
20. _____

Now comes the interesting part. When you exchange lists with your boss, how many criteria will be the same on both of your lists? For the sake of discussion, assume that both you and your boss listed twenty criteria. Would you agree on 19 or 20 out of 20? Research indicates (and our experience confirms) that only one of one hundred employees would agree with their boss on 19 or 20 out of 20 criteria. Would you agree on 15 out of 20 criteria? About twenty-five out of one hundred employees would agree with their boss on 15 out of 20 criteria. How about 10 out of 20? Usually fifty out of one hundred employees would agree on 10 out of the 20 criteria. What about 5 out of 20? About twenty out of one hundred employees would agree on 5 out of 20 criteria. For no agreement at all or agreement on only 1 out of 20, less than one out of one hundred managers would have this level of agreement (or disagreement).

Table 3.2. Amount of agreement between boss-employee pairs on performance criteria.

Number of criteria found on both lists	Frequency of occurrence
19 or 20 out of 20	less than 1%
15 out of 20	about 25%
10 out of 20	about 50%
5 out of 20	about 20%
0 or 1 out of 20	less than 1%

The responses cited in the example above suggest that we may have a relatively weak grasp on what our boss considers most important about our job, and that our employees may have little idea of what we expect of them. In fact, there is probably more confusion over performance criteria and their accompanying standards than over any other part of the performance appraisal process.

Consider the following example. Your organization uses the evaluation form presented in Table 3.3. You are familiar with the form; your boss is familiar with the form. What else is necessary? Probably quite a few things. For starters, how do you define quality in terms of your job? What do you mean by quality? What is included under the heading job knowledge? What is meant by working relationships? Are the criteria listed on the form appropriate criteria for evaluating you in your job? Do the criteria include all of the more important facets of your job? Are all of the criteria relevant and central to your job? Do the criteria help you in setting priorities? If these questions can be answered with positive responses, then you have a workable set of criteria. However, experience shows that, for most employees, undefined criteria such as quality, quantity, etc. detract from, rather than enhance, the appraisal process.

Table 3.3. Example of an incomplete appraisal form.

Employee's Name _____ Date _____

Position _____ Supervisor _____

Review period: From _____ to _____

Criteria	Comments	Rating
1. Quality of Work		
2. Quantity of Work		
3. Job Knowledge		
4. Working Relationships		
5. Supervisory Skills (For supervisors only)		

Definitions of Performance Rating Categories

5. Outstanding   The employee has exceeded all of the performance expectations for this criterion and has made many significant contributions to the efficiency and economy of this organization through such performance.
4. Exceeds Expectations   The employee regularly works beyond a majority of the performance expectations of this criterion and has made significant contributions to the efficiency and economy of this organization through such performance.
3. Satisfactory   The employee has met the performance expectations for this criterion and has contributed to the efficiency and economy of this organization.
2. Needs Improvement   The employee has failed to meet one or more of the significant performance expectations for this criterion.
1. Unsatisfactory   The employee has failed to meet the performance expectations for this criterion

Comments:

Employee Signature   **Supervisor Signature**

How can this problem of undefined and unknown criteria be resolved? The answer is simple: you and your boss must meet together in order to hammer out a list of criteria that will accurately reflect your job. We're not suggesting that you like, or even necessarily agree with, the criteria. But you do have the "right" to know in advance what the criteria are so that you can use them to guide your performance. The following example illustrates this point.

Case 3.1

An engineer was assigned to a unit where he had never worked before. The unit had many long staff meetings which could not start until he arrived with the most recent drawings. Punctuality was not his forte—he usually arrived at the staff meetings ten to fifteen minutes late. His boss mentioned a couple of times that it would be nice if he could arrive at the appointed hour so that they could start the meeting on time. This went on for about nine months. At the annual performance review covering this period, the boss gave this engineer an overall rating of "needs improvement," citing a "refusal to contribute fully to the team effort as evidenced by a continued lack of concern for getting to meetings on time."

The engineer was livid when he read this. He complained that punctuality was a completely inappropriate factor for rating a professional engineer. His boss argued, in return, that his lack of punctuality had wasted over one hour per week of the other professionals' time while they were cooling their heels waiting for him to arrive. The engineer's final comment was that he could probably have arrived at the meetings on time if he had known how important it was to his boss that he show up on time.

This case exemplifies a key issue. First, a question: Is it legitimate for a professional manager to evaluate another professional on punctuality? The answer is an obvious "yes," if punctuality is important for successful performance. Does the manager have the obligation of telling the engineer in specific terms that he will be evaluated on punctuality? Many managers will argue this point, but again we believe the answer is "yes." The manager has a right to expect the engineer to arrive on time, but the manager also has an obligation to inform the engineer that, since the engineer is having a problem with being punctual, he will be evaluated on punctuality. This case illustrates the importance of defining performance critera in advance. If the engineer had been aware of the criterion of punctuality, he could have used this information to change his behavior. The purpose of performace criteria, after all, is not to punish an employee for inadequate performance, but to provide guidelines for successful performance. The engineer could have chosen to ignore this criterion, of course; but the choice would have been his. Learning the criteria after the fact negates any opportunity to change one's performance for that appraisal period.

Case 3.2

There is a popular oil filter commercial on television right now. The mechanic slides out from beneath a car, shakes his head, and begins to figure out the cost for a new engine. The mechanic looks up and comments, "You can pay me now—a few dollars for an oil filter—or you can pay me later—many dollars for a new engine." The same can be said for performance criteria. You can pay the relatively low psychological cost of discussing the evaluation criteria before the appraisal period starts, or you can pay the substantially highter psychological cost later of a heated discussion over what the criteria were that led to this less-than-favorable appraisal.

After the criteria have been discussed and agreed upon, the next step in the process is to prioritize the criteria. Rarely are all criteria of equal importance. This being the case, it makes good sense for the boss and employee to review the criteria with an eye to ranking them in terms of their overall importance. Again, while the boss's ranking may not match the subordinate's own priorities, the subordinate can use the boss's ranking as information to guide his or her decisions about on-the-job behavior. The case cited below is an excellent example of this process in action.

Case 3.3

After the production manager and the plant supervisor determined the eighteen criteria for evaluating the plant supervisor's performance, they reviewed the criteria and grouped them into three major categories: (1) most important, (2) secondary importance, and (3) to be accomplished as time permits. The plant supervisor was surprised to see that the production manager placed compliance with the affirmative action plan in the "most important" category. The production manager explained that the plant had failed to meet its affirmative action goals for six out of the last eight quarters and that including this criterion in the "most important" category would help emphasize its urgency, thereby increasing the chance of improved performance in this category. The additional step of prioritizing the criteria clarified this point for the plant supervisor.

A Dilemma

The process of developing performance criteria illustrates a point that may not be obvious to the casual observer. The process forces us to develop criteria for particular jobs, or for groups of jobs known as job families. There is no single set of criteria that are equally applicable to each and every job within an organization, or even within a department, for that matter. If we ask ourselves, "Should a department head and a secretary be appraised on the same criteria? Should an industrial engineer and an accountant be evaluated on the same criteria?", surely the answer to both questions is obvious. If we attempt to develop a uniform set of criteria that apply equally well to a wide range of jobs, we end up with a rating form that resembles that presented in Table 3.3.

As the preceding discussion illustrates, this form has some serious problems. What specifically is meant by "quality of work"? What is "quantity of work"?

How will "job knowledge" be defined? What is included under "working conditions"? Which "supervisory skills" should be evaluated? Yet another difficulty is the fact that quantity, quality, and job knowledge are often intimately entwined in the performance of the job. For example, is budgeting ability quantity? Is it quality? Is it job knowledge? It's probably all three. Case 3.4 examplifies this point.

Case 3.4

A clerk-typist was working with his boss to develop performance criteria for his job using the form presented in Table 3.3. Under "quality of work," he thought that he should be evaluated on typing ability, filing ability, and accuracy of forms. Under "quantity of work," he listed typing ability, filing ability, number of forms completed, and mail sorting. Under "job knowledge," he included typing ability, knowledge of departmental filing system, knowledge of departmental forms, and knowledge of departmental policies and procedures. At this point he grew frustrated with the process as he realized that he was recording many of the same rating factors under every criterion.

If your organization, like most organizations, needs to limit its number of appraisal forms, there is no reason for despair. It is possible to develop a single form that can be tailored to a wide variety of different jobs. Later in this chapter we have presented such a form (See Table 3.10).

Performance Criteria—A Summary

Formulating performance criteria is the first step in the performance appraisal process. These criteria should be specific, job-related factors and not a mere listing of personality traits, attitudes, or other factors which cannot be assessed. The criteria must represent all important components of the job and must include all factors essential for success on that job. Since the subordinate's perspective on the job will probably be slightly different from the boss's perspective, the very fact of involving the subordinate in the development of the performance criteria for his job goes a long way towards assuring that the system will be perceived as fair.

Table 3.4 illustrates the criteria that were developed by one group of managers in response to the question, "What factors, tasks, abilities, criteria, accountabilities, etc. should be used for evaluating your performance?" This list is presented as an elaborate example of what can be done by a group of people who are interested in developing a more effective approach to performance appraisal.

Table 3.4. Example of criteria developed by a group of managers.

Criterion	Definition

Planning: Setting objectives, budgeting, scheduling, forecasting.
Time management: Meeting deadlines. Leaving time for special projects and contingencies.
Organization: Planning and organizing own and/or other's work for most effective handling or reduction of unnecessary activities.
Human relations: Work relationships with supervisor, peers, others outside working unit.
Monitoring/evaluation: Keeping track of people, projects, and equipment to assure performance standards.
Customer relations: Developing personal relations with customers. Meeting with customers to review products to meet their needs. Handling complaints about products and services.
Communications—written: Effectiveness of reports, letters, memos, etc.
Communications—verbal: Effectiveness of oral communications; listening skills.
Leadership: Skills in orienting, motivating, and guiding others.
Cost awareness: Awareness of financial impact of decisions and actions.
Development of people: Recognizing growth potential; coaching and counseling skills.
Affirmative action: Working with others harmoniously without regard to race, religion, national origin, sex, age, or handicap. Support of organizational Equal Employment Opportunity objectives and timetables.
Staffing: Recruiting, screening, interviewing, and selecting applicants
Decision making: Making timely decision considering relevant factors and evaluating alternatives.
Personnel practices: Use of salary benefits programs, performance appraisal program, career planning, training and development opportunities, etc.
Personal growth and development: Awareness of own strengths and weaknesses; plans for elimination of deficiencies; attends training activities; keeps abreast of new developments.

PERFORMANCE STANDARDS

Once you have completed the first two steps in the appraisal process—developing performance criteria and prioritizing them—you are well on your way towards an effective appraisal system. Even if you stopped the process at this point, you would still have an appraisal process that is better than most, because it has been personalized to the level of the employee being evaluated. However, to maximize the value of your appraisal system, you need to take it a step further; you need to develop performance standards or expectations for each of the criteria.

Many appraisal systems beg the question of performance standards by referring to "standards" or "expectations" while never actually defining what the standards or expectations are. An example of this can be found in Table 3.3. If you glance at the bottom of the form, you will note that there are definitions for each of the performance rating categories. Look at the definition for "satisfactory"— "The employee has met the performance expectations for this criterion and has contributed to the efficiency and economy of this organization." This definition leaves one major term undefined—"performance expectations." Before a rater can use this form in a meaningful way, he or she must first know what the performance expectations are. This is especially true in those instances where the employee is rated "Needs Improvement." Telling an employee that he or she has failed to meet one or more of the significant performance expectations for this criterion without defining what the performance expectations are does not qualify for the "Effective Feedback of the Year" award. In fact, a less-than-satisfactory rating that is not supported by specific instances of poor performance will probably create hostility, resentment, or at least confusion in the employee, and thus will defeat the purpose of performance appraisal: understanding.

Case 3.5

An employee presented the next fiscal year's budget and supporting documents to her boss. The boss reviewed the material and returned it to the employee with a note reading: "I don't like it; why don't you put this attempt aside and start from scratch?" The employee, who had put her best effort into the preparation of the original budget, approached her boss for some pointers on what to use in her next attempt. When she asked him what was wrong with the report, he responded, "Any competent manager should be able to figure that out!" Now she knew that not only was her budget not acceptable, in addition she was incompetent. And she still did not understand what the boss wanted in a budget!

DEVELOPING PERFORMANCE STANDARDS

Performance criteria are not complete until accompanied by performance standards or expectations. The performance standard is the response to the question, "How good is good?" (or "How bad is bad?"). More specifically, the performance standards define the various levels of performance for each criterion. For example, if your rating system has three levels of performance: "Needs Improvement," "Meets Expectations," and "Outstanding," then performance standards are needed to define each of these levels.

Many managers assume that performance standards cannot be established for those criteria that do not measure countable things such as profitability, board feet of lumber, percentage scrap, return on investment, number of units serviced, etc. This assumption could not be further from the truth. The majority of criteria used to evaluate the performance of most employees are not a question of "countables." They describe specific behaviors or actions which differentiate levels of performance. If we can answer the question of what someone who is superior at budgeting does that the mediocre employee does not do, we have begun to define our performance standard for outstanding performance in budgeting. If we can answer the question of what is satisfactory scheduling for a staffing coordinator, then we have begun to define a performance standard for satisfactory performance in the area of scheduling.

If we cannot answer the question of what characterizes satisfactory performance on a particular criterion, then how will we ever be able to evaluate performance in terms of that criterion? We always evaluate against some standard. Without a standard, it is impossible to do any kind of effective appraisal.

Another function of performance standards is a teaching role. When an employee has a clear idea of what you require in a budget for it to be acceptable, preparing a budget that meets your expectations is far more likely to occur. It becomes more than a hit-and-miss proposition wherein we learn the right way by first doing it the wrong way a number of times.

We had the opportunity to assist a group of managers in developing specific performance standards for their jobs. Two of the criteria for which they developed performance standards were presented earlier in Figure 2.5. These examples may be more elaborate than the performance standards you will develop with your boss and subordinates, but they exemplify what can be done, even with a criterion as seemingly amorphous as "Accepting Responsibility and Initiating Action."

Table 3.10, presented later in this chapter, presents an appraisal format that lends itself to either of two situations:(1) Settings where there is only one person performing a particular job in an organization with the resulting criteria and standards unique to that individual and (2) Settings where the criteria and standards are applicable to groups of employees.

Developing Criteria and Standards for Groups of Employees

For some groups within organizations, it is appropriate to develop criteria for the group as a whole instead of developing criteria for each employee individually. If employees in a particular group have significant similarity in their job duties and functions, that group would be a good candidate for common criteria and standards. The potential groups of employees are many in most organizations. Some of the groups, or job families, that have used the approach to be described on the following pages include: mid-level managers, bank tellers, office assistants, research technicians, librarians, engineers, custodians, police officers, production employees, supervisors, and public utility workers. Actual criteria and standards developed with some of these groups are presented in the Appendix.

There are two approaches that can be used to develop criteria and standards for a job family. The first approach utilizes a task-force comprised of job holders and supervisors to develop the criteria and standards through a series of meetings. The second approach is to use a series of questionnaires and survey job incumbents and supervisors. We have seen organizations use every possible combination of these two approaches and arrive at a good set of criteria and standards.

In the next section we have presented a series of questionnaires that can be used to develop performance criteria and standards for a job family. The technical name for this process of developing criteria and standards is the behaviorally anchored approach. This term derives from the fact that we are attempting to define (or anchor) our performance standards with examples of performance (or job behavior). Hence the name behavioral anchor.

Questionnaires for Groups of Employees

Step 1. *Identifying Job Factors, Tasks, and Abilities.*

For each job or job family (e.g., clerk-typists), survey job incumbents and supervisors to identify the job factors, tasks and abilities that should be included in a performance review. This step is crucial: the job-relatedness and validity of the method require that we begin the process by focusing on the job. If there are only a few job incumbents, then they should all be polled. If there are over 30 incumbents, poll only a sample. The sample questionnaire below was used to develop a list of job factors for a group of department heads. This questionnaire is an example for purposes of illustration and should be changed to describe the job or job family actually being surveyed.

Table 3.5 Questionnaire for *Step 1* **of the behavioral anchor approach**

Name: _____ Department: _____

This is the first questionnaire concerning the development of performance standards for **department heads.** In the spaces below we would like you to record those factors, tasks or abilities that should be used for evaluating the performance of the department head. Try to stay away from things that cannot be directly measured such as attitudes or personality traits. Focus on those things that can be measured or observed and that are related to the job.

For example, some possible factors might include:

    Long range planning skills
    Budgeting
    Meeting deadlines and other commitments
    Development of staff

In the spaces below, please list those factors that you think should be considered when rating the performance of department heads:

1. _____
2. _____
3. _____
4. _____
5. _____
6. _____
7. _____
8. _____
9. _____
10. _____
11. _____
12. _____
13. _____
14. _____
15. _____

If more space is required, use the back of this form.

Step 2. *Selecting 25 Most Important Job Factors*

Job factors and tasks identified in Step 1 are taken from all the responding employee questionnaires and combined into one master list (omitting duplications and overlapping items). This list is used to prepare a second questionnaire which is then sent to all job incumbents and their supervisors. In this questionnaire, an example of which follows, they are asked to select the 25 most important elements which should be included in a performance review for the department head position.

Table 3.6 Questionnaire for *Step 2* **of the behavioral anchor approach**

Name: _____ Department: _____

This is the second questionnaire in the development of a behaviorally anchored performance evaluation scale. We have listed and combined your responses from Questionnaire No. 1 and now we would like you to select, from the factors listed below, 25 and only 25 factors that you believe to be *most important* in evaluating the performance of department heads. Place a check in the space to the left of the factors you select. Please complete this questionnaire and return it to _____ by _____ .

REMEMBER: Select only 25 factors.

_____ 1. Ability to conduct meetings
_____ 2. Ability to delegate authority
_____ 3. Attention to detail
_____ 4. Knowledge of programming
_____ 5. Employee development
_____ 6. Cooperation
_____ 7. Employee performance evaluation
_____ 8. Budgeting skills
_____ 9. Coordinating skills
_____ 10. Work assignment techniques
_____ 11. Commitment to department goals
_____ 12. Communication skills—oral
_____ 13. Communication skills—written
_____ 14. Decision making skills
_____ 15. System design skills
_____ 16. Cost awareness
_____ 17. Creativity
_____ 18. Team development skills
_____ 19. Staffing and hiring skills
_____ 20. Flexibility and adaptability
_____ 21. Organizing skills
_____ 22. Accepting responsibility and initiating action
_____ 23. Counseling/coaching of subordinates
_____ 24. Interpersonal skills
_____ 25. Job knowledge
_____ 26. Management by objectives
_____ 27. Client contact and service
_____ 28. Safety/loss control
_____ 29. Communication with upper management
_____ 30. Participation
_____ 31. Time management skills
_____ 32. Development of subordinates
_____ 33. Problem solving skills
_____ 34. Work habits
_____ 35. Stability
_____ 36. Meeting deadlines/commitments
_____ 37. Organizing skills
_____ 38. Professional development
_____ 39. Personal development
_____ 40. Setting objectives
_____ 41. Meeting objectives
_____ 42. Planning-long range
_____ 43. Planning-short range
_____ 44. Policy formulation
_____ 45. Encouraging ideas
_____ 46. Relations with associates
_____ 47. Technical competence
_____ 48. Supervision of subordinates
_____ 49. Troubleshooting skills
_____ 50. Cost reduction skills

Step 3. Defining Job Criteria.

Retain and define those criteria selected by most of the job incumbents and supervisors. Usually a criterion is retained if 60% of the incumbents selected it. However, 60% is simply a rule-of-thumb and one should feel free to go as high or low as necessary with percentage of responses to get enough criteria. Step 3 may result in as few as 11 or 12 job factors or as many as 25 or 26. After selecting the criteria, *each one must be defined* to ensure that all the raters are referring to the same thing. For example, rather than just listing the word "creativity," use a definition similar to the following:

> *Showing Creativity on the Job:* This job aspect involves recognizing problems not yielding to present methods of solution: identifying the relationships between key elements involved; identifying solutions and sharing them with others; and implementing the solutions to be sure they truly solve the various problems.

The process used to define each of the criteria identified in the second step is fairly straightforward. The person coordinating the development of the performance evaluation instrument should turn to the dictionary, lexicon, and/or textbooks to construct preliminary definitions for each of the criteria. If the organization has a position classification plan or has done job analysis for test development, those instruments may have useful definitions. After definitions have been drafted, they should be reviewed by a select number of job incumbents and supervisors to assure that they are complete, reflect actual job duties and conditions, and that they do not include unnecessary verbiage. The section on definitions is usually two or three typewritten lines in length.

Some sample definitions for job criteria developed by one organization for a management performance evaluation instrument are as follows:

> *Oral Communications:* This criterion involves clear expression of thoughts and ideas; ability to listen and share information; understanding replies or directions from others.
>
> *Written Communications:* This criterion involves composition of reports, letters, memos, proposals, and other documents; use of principles of writing such as clarity, brevity, accuracy, and logic.
>
> *Decision-Making and Problem Solving:* This criterion involves specific definition of the problem, assembly of available information, data or facts; review, analysis, and evaluation of the information; formulation of alternatives; application of logic and decision making principles in selecting a decision or solution from among the options; sharing the decision with others as appropriate.

Step 4. Producing Performance Standards or Expectations

For each retained criterion, ask job incumbents and supervisors for examples of: (1) Performance that meets job standards for this criterion; (2) Outstanding performance on this criterion; (3) Performance that falls below job standards for this criterion. The easiest way to get this information is to list separately each criterion and its definition at the top of a sheet of paper. If there were 20 criteria selected in Step 2, then this questionnaire process would require 20 separate sheets of paper. A sample of a questionnaire for one criterion is presented below. Remember there will be as many pages as job criteria. One way to simplify this step is to divide the different job criteria questionnaires among supervisor and incumbents to avoid having everyone generating examples for all the criteria.

Table 3.7 Questionnaire for *Step 4* **of the behavioral anchor approach**

Name: _____ Department: _____

This is the third questionnaire concerning the development of a behaviorally anchored evaluation scale for department heads. (There will be one short questionnaire after this one.) In this developmental phase *we are producing the actual behavioral anchors* (numerical values) to be used for each of the job criteria developed in the first two questionnaires.

On the following pages we have listed those criteria (job factors) you have selected as being most important for evaluating the performance of a department head. We have listed one criterion per page. For each of the criteria we would like you to think of an example which answers each of the following questions:

1. What behavior indicates that job standards are being met?

2. What behavior is indicative of outstanding performance for this job factor?

3. What behavior represents below-standard job performance?

Answer *each* of these questions for *every* job factor or criterion.

For example, let's say that you were answering the three questions for the following criterion:

CRITERION: MEETING DEADLINES AND OTHER COMMITMENTS: This element involves the number of deadlines met and commitments kept: planning and scheduling to get expected results within allocated times; advance anticipation of problems in meeting deadlines or keeping commitments; dependability in meeting deadlines.

1. What behavior indicates meeting the job standard?

EXAMPLE: This person can be expected to have work done on the day that it is due.

2. What behavior is indicative of outstanding performance for this job factor?

EXAMPLE: This person can be expected to have reports, projects, or tasks completed far enough before their deadline to allow time to review them and make revisions.

3. What behavior represents below-standard job performance?

EXAMPLE: This person often misses deadlines and commitments. This person needs constant reminders in order to meet deadlines.

Please allow yourself enough time to complete this questionnaire. It will probably take you between one and four hours to generate the behavioral anchors for all of the job criteria. If you wish, you may list more than one behavioral example when answering the three questions.

Step 5. Rating Performance Examples

A number of performance examples have now been generated for each job factor (criterion). Depending on how many job incumbents and supervisors participated in Step 4, there may be only eight or ten performance examples per job factor, or there may be as many as sixty or seventy. In the sample questionnaire above (Table 3.7), three performance examples were identified for the job criterion, **Meeting deadlines and other commitments.**

In this final step, all the performance examples (the standard, the outstanding, and the below-standard) for each job factor are compiled in one list. Job incumbents and supervisors then rate each of the performance examples on a poor to good (1 to 5) performance scale. Table 3.8 defines the five-point scale.

Table 3.8 Rating scale and values for rating performance examples

1. *Unacceptable Performance.* The "1" employee is unsatisfactory. The unit would be much better off without this level of performance.
2. *Below Job Standards.* The "2" employee needs to improve. The "2" employee exceeds the "1" since he is of some help to the unit.
3. *Meets Job Standards.* The "3" employee performs the job satisfactorily.
4. *Exceeds Job Standards.* The "4" employee goes beyond the routine accomplishment of the job.
5. *Outstanding Performance.* The "5" employee far exceeds the job standards. He is one of the top performers in the unit.

Performance examples are eliminated when fewer than 60% of the job incumbents and supervisors agree on a particular numerical rating. For example, the five-point scale presented in Table 3.8 was used to rate the following behavioral statement:

"This person is willing to work overtime whenever needed."

Job incumbents and supervisors rated the above statement as follows: 20% gave it a rating of 5 (or outstanding performance); 68% gave it a rating of 4 (exceeds the job standard); 12% gave it a rating of 3 (meets the job standard). Since more than 60% of the raters gave this item a rating value of 4, it would be retained. Table 3.9 below displays a sample questionnaire for assigning numerical values to selected performance examples of a single job criterion.

Table 3.9 Performance examples suggested by job incumbents and supervisors for one job criterion (for the position of department head).

CRITERION: ACCEPTING RESPONSIBILITY AND INITIATING ACTION. This aspect of the job involves the amount of personal responsibility taken for the completion of work, the amount of work progress made without complete supervisory direction, the willingness to think through work barriers and to keep working towards priority goals, and to follow-up on work that seems necessary to achieve job (or unit) goals.

DIRECTIONS—PLEASE USE THE RATING SCALE VALUES PRESENTED IN TABLE 3.8 TO RATE EACH OF THE PERFORMANCE EXAMPLES LISTED BELOW AS IT RELATES TO THE ABOVE CRITERION. RECORD YOUR RATING IN THE BLANK SPACE TO THE LEFT OF EACH BEHAVIORAL EXAMPLE.

BEHAVIORAL EXAMPLES

_____ 1. Dedicated and does an outstanding job in new and different situations
_____ 2. Readily accepts new or different tasks
_____ 3. Tends to ignore new findings, techniques, and procedures
_____ 4. Panics and/or leaves new or different situations
_____ 5. Willing to use new findings or ideas only if they are proven to him/her
_____ 6. Responds to crisis events quickly and effectively
_____ 7. Recognizes the new and different and takes appropriate action
_____ 8. Knows and applies new findings, developments, or technology
_____ 9. Flexible in responding to the new and different
_____ 10. Consistently profits from new, unexpected and difficult situations
_____ 11. Knows when to seek out someone more qualified to help
_____ 12. Needs constant supervision in new or different situations
_____ 13. Jumps to erroneous conclusions or actions in new situations
_____ 14. Incorporates changes and new developments into work to speed accomplishment
_____ 15. Needs instruction or training but then adapts to new situations readily.
_____ 16. Becomes bogged down or disorganized in new situations.
_____ 17. Will not or cannot adapt to changing procedures
_____ 18. Recognizes and avoids potential problems in new situations
_____ 19. Is far ahead of peers in using new findings, techniques, or procedures
_____ 20. Feels anything new is a threat to his/her security
_____ 21. Always looking for a way to avoid the new or different
_____ 22. Approaches new problems or situations with inappropriate methods

At this point, then, employees and supervisors have assigned numerical values (scale of 1 to 5) to each performance example for each job factor (Table 3.9). With the results from this step, the *final* actual numerical value to each performance example can be assiged (60% of the respondents must agree). The various job factors are then reordered (one per page) with the performance examples listed in the numerically rated sequence from five to zero. Figure 2.5, presented earlier, illustrates this. Remember there will be from ten to twenty pages like Table 3.9 for each job or job family in your organization, since there will be ten to twenty job factors or criteria for each job or job family.

At performance evaluation time, the rater's task is to review the behavioral anchors presented for each job factor (arrived at through the 5-step process outlined above) and to select that level of performance which *best describes* the performance of the person being rated. For example, if the rater were using Figure 2.5., he would determine if the statements listed under "5" were most typical of the person being rated, or if the "4" statements were more descriptive, etc. The rater may not find statements that describe exactly the person being rated. However, the rater is expected to use the statements given as reference points which will guide his or her ratings, and choose one statement which comes closest to describing the performance of the ratee.

Time Requirements

For a single job family of 20 or more employees, the criteria and standards approach requires about 10 to 20 days for someone to coordinate collecting the information, two or three days of clerical time, and four to eight hours for each of the job holders and supervisors who participate in the developmental effort. The five steps outlined in the preceding section will take approximately three months from start to finish. This allows time to send and receive questionnaires and time for incumbents to respond.

It is possible to conduct the five steps using groups of job holders and supervisors. If you wish to use the group approach, plan at least five group meetings. Steps One and Two can be accomplished during the first meeting in 2 to 3 hours. Step Three can take as long as 12 hours. Steps Four and Five can be done in about 3 hours.

Developing Additional Criteria and Standards

In many cases employees who have identical job titles are nevertheless involved in different projects or assigned special tasks. To take account of these differences, once criteria have been developed for a group of employees, we should return to our original question and ensure that the evaluation process is still personalized by asking, "Are there any additional criteria, not included on the list developed by/for the group, that this employee should be evaluated on?" This is often the case for managers. In recognition of this fact, many organizations include space for additional criteria on their rating forms.

A Sample Rating Form

Table 3.10 on the following pages presents a sample of an evaluation form that can be used for either employee-specific or job-specific criteria. In addition to space for the criteria and standards, the form also includes a series of essay questions which focus on employee development issues. These essay questions are discussed at greater length in subsequent chapters.

Table 3.10. Example of a multi-purpose performance appraisal form.

Performance evaluation
Annual review

EMPLOYEE NAME _____ DATE OF EVALUATION _____

POSITION TITLE _____ EVAULATION PERIOD

LOCATION _____ FROM ___/___/___ TO ___/___/___

In the spaces below list the criteria you developed with the employee and recorded on the performance standards worksheet. Rate each of the criteria using the performance standards you listed on the performance standards worksheet. Be sure to include comments.

RATING SCALE

5—OUTSTANDING   2—NEEDS IMPROVEMENT

3—MEETS EXPECTATIONS

4—EXCEEDS EXPECTATIONS   1—UNSATISFACTORY

NA—NOT APPLICABLE OR NO OPPORTUNITY TO OBSERVE

CRITERIA   **RATING**

1. _____ ☐
   COMMENTS

2. _____ ☐
   COMMENTS

3. _____ ☐
   COMMENTS

4. _____ ☐
   COMMENTS

5. _____ ☐
   COMMENTS

6. _____ ☐
   COMMENTS

Table 3.10—*Continued*

CRITERIA	RATING

7. _____ ☐
COMMENTS

8. _____ ☐
COMMENTS

9. _____ ☐
COMMENTS

10. _____ ☐
COMMENTS

11. _____ ☐
COMMENTS

12. _____ ☐
COMMENTS

13. _____ ☐
COMMENTS

14. _____ ☐
COMMENTS

15. _____ ☐
COMMENTS

16. _____ ☐
COMMENTS

17. _____ ☐
COMMENTS

Table 3.10—*Continued*

CRITERIA   **RATING**

18. _____ ☐
COMMENTS

19. _____ ☐
COMMENTS

HERE ARE WHAT I SEE AS YOUR MAJOR STRENGTHS AND ABILITIES, THE THINGS YOU'VE DONE PARTICULARLY WELL, AND THE SIGNIFICANT IMPROVEMENTS YOU'VE MADE SINCE YOUR LAST EVALUATION:

I THINK IMPROVEMENT IN THESE AREAS WILL INCREASE YOUR OVERALL EFFECTIVENESS ON THE JOB: (EXPLAIN)

Table 3.10—*Continued*

I ALSO CONSIDERED THESE ADDITIONAL FACTORS (IF ANY) IN REACHING THE OVERALL PERFORMANCE RATING:

OVERALL PERFORMANCE

HERE'S HOW I RATE YOUR OVERALL PERFORMANCE, BASED ON THE PERFORMANCE CRITERIA WE ESTABLISHED AND CONSIDERING THE RELATIVE IMPORTANCE OF EACH: ☐

DEVELOPMENTAL PLAN

WHAT STEPS SHOULD BE TAKEN TO MAINTAIN OR IMPROVE YOUR PERFORMANCE OR TO HELP YOU PROGRESS TOWARD YOUR PERSONAL CAREER OBJECTIVES?

Table 3.10—*Continued*

EMPLOYEE COMMENTS

EMPLOYEE SIGNATURE — **DATE**

(Signature indicates you have seen and discussed this appraisal with your supervisor. It does not necessarily imply agreement with the appraisal or overall rating.)

SUPERVISOR'S SIGNATURE — **DATE**

REVIEWED BY — **DATE**

ADDITIONAL REVIEW *(If any)* — **DATE**

CHAPTER

4

Protecting Employee Rights: Avoiding Rater Errors

In the last fifteen to twenty years there has been increasing attention paid to the legal rights of employees in the work place. A formidable body of legislation, administrative law, and court and arbitration rulings have increasingly reinforced the right of employees to be treated fairly by their employers. Granted that some employees' complaints of discrimination or of other mistreatment have been the malicious brew of sour grapes, or simply frivolous, we must recognize that the current body of regulation is a response to very real abuses of the past. It is safe to assume that restrictions will, if anything, increase.

The United States is still relatively free of constraints on the actions of managers, however. While in Stockholm, one of the authors met with the president of a major Swedish corporation. The corporation's management was in the process of negotiating the next year's operating budget with the employees as required by Swedish law. In many areas, Swedish labor legislation has granted unions authority to review many management decisions, effectively removing management's right to manage. Although such a situation is not foreseen for the United States, management's insensitivity to employee rights and needs suggests that here, as in Sweden, such extensive constraints may come to pass if present conditions go ignored. Therefore, the United States manager should have a working knowledge of existing constraints, if for no more lofty motive than self-interest.

The reader has probably heard of the federal legislation concerning nondiscrimination in the selection (hiring) of employees. However, many managers are not aware that the same body of legislation pertains to performance appraisal systems.

The legislation most profoundly affecting the practice of performance appraisal stems from the Civil Rights Act of 1964, specifically Title VII of that Act. Title VII was initially directed toward discriminatory employee selection practices, but development of case law over the years has broadened interpretation of the Act considerably, to now include performance appraisal systems.

The body of law impacting performance appraisal practices is growing so rapidly that probably only attorneys specializing in labor law can be completely current. Managers need not be "legal beagles," of course, but they must have at least a general idea of trends in the law. To that end, we have summarized a few of the more important cases relating to performance appraisal.

Griggs v. Duke Power (1971)[1]

This was the first Supreme Court decision related to Title VII. Duke Power Company had one department composed entirely of blacks, while other departments were entirely white.

A high school diploma or a satisfactory score on two aptitude tests was required for employment in the white departments, thus excluding blacks (usually on the basis of the aptitude tests).

The court's decision explicitly endorsed the Equal Employment Opportunity Commission guidelines, and ruled that all employment criteria that adversely affect a class member (e.g., racial minorities and women) must be shown to be job related.

The decision also stated that it is equally illegal to discriminate against nonminority groups:

> "Congress did not intend by Title VII, to guarantee a job to every person regardless of their qualifications. In short, the Act does not command that a person be hired simply because he was formerly the subject of discrimination or because he is a member of a minority group. Discriminatory preferences for any group, minority or majority, are precisely and only what the Congress has proscribed."

Rowe v. General Motors (1972)[2]

The Fifth Circuit Court of Appeals ruled that reliance upon all-white supervisory recommendations based upon subjective and vague standards had resulted in discrimination against blacks in the promotion process.

The court noted that, in addition to subjective and vague standards, supervisors were given no written instructions regarding qualifications necessary for promotion, hourly employees were not notified of promotional opportunities, and there were no safeguards in the promotion procedure to prevent discriminatory practices.

Brito vs. Zia Company (1973)[3]

When Zia had laid off a number of Spanish-surnamed employees, the 10th Circuit Court of Appeals found it in violation of Title VII. The court stated that the company had not demonstrated that the appraisal instrument was related to important elements of the jobs being evaluated. The court also concluded that

---

1. Griggs v. Duke Power Company, 401 U.S. (1971), 3 EDP 8137
2. Rowe v. General Motors Corporative Extension Service, 372 F. Sup. 126 (1974).
3. Brito v. Zia Co., 478 F.2nd 1200 (1973).

the evaluations were based on subjective supervisory observations that resulted in a disproportionately high number of terminations of employees with Spanish surnames.

Wade v. Mississippi Cooperative Extension Service (1974)[4]

The Fifth Circuit Court of Appeals held that what the organization presented as an objective appraisal of job performance was in fact based on ratings of such general traits as loyalty to the organization, outlook on life, capacity for growth, and ethnic habits.

The defendant was unable to show that the criteria were job related.

Texas Department of Community Affairs vs. Burdine (1981)[5]

The plaintiff, a female employee of the Texas Department of Community Affairs, charged sex discrimination when a male employee was selected for a supervisory position that the plaintiff had applied for. A staff reduction occurred at about the time the supervisory position was filled, and the plaintiff was terminated. The plaintiff also alleged sex discrimination in the termination. A lower court held that the company had not discriminated in either the promotion or termination action. However, on appeal, the Fifth Circuit Court of Appeals reversed the lower court's decision regarding the termination, stating that the company bears the burden of proving that the employment action was made for nondiscriminatory reasons.

The Supreme Court rejected the appellate court's reasoning, however, stating:

> "The ultimate burden of persuading (the court) that the defendant intentionally discriminated against the plaintiff remains *at all times with the plaintiff.*" (emphasis added)
>
> ". . . we have stated consistently that the employee's *prima facia* case of discrimination will be rebutted if the employer articulates lawful reasons for the action. . . ."

The Supreme Court then addressed the promotion decision:

> "The Court of Appeals also erred in requiring the defendant to prove by objective evidence that the person hired or promoted was more qualified than the plaintiff . . . it is the plaintiff's task to demonstrate that similarly situated employees were not treated fairly."

This last case reaffirms the stance taken by the Supreme Court all along—namely, that in cases of alleged discrimination, the burden of proof lies with the plaintiff. The organization is not obliged to prove that it did not discriminate.

---

4. Wade v. Mississippi Cooperative Extension Service, 372 F. Sup. 126 (1974).
5. Texas Department of Community Affairs v. Burdine, 25 FEP 79–1764 (1981).

ENFORCEMENT OF TITLE VII

There are two federal agencies as well as numerous state and local agencies that monitor compliance with Title VII.

Equal Employment Opportunity Commission (EEOC)

The EEOC is the most visible and best-known monitoring agency, at least to the general public. Its jurisdiction encompasses the practices and records of organizations that employ 15 or more people over 20 or more weeks.

EEOC does not have the power to order an organization to halt the practices believed to be discriminatory but it *can* subpoena and question witnesses under oath, and present evidence to courts of alleged discrimination.

EEOC must defer to a state fair employment practice commission before initiating its own investigation, but *after* a charge has been filed with the state agency, EEOC may begin its own investigation, and is not bound by the findings of the local agency.

Office of Federal Contract Compliance Programs (OFCCP)

The OFCCP has the right to investigate personnel policies of any employer who holds a federal contract of $10,000 or more. All federal contracts of $10,000 or more contain clauses requiring the contractors and subcontractors to refrain from engaging in discriminatory practices.

Unlike the EEOC, the OFCCP does have some enforcement power. If OFCCP determines that there has been a violation of the nondiscriminatory clauses of a contract, it can cancel the contract, bar the employer from bidding on other federal contracts until they are in compliance, and recommend that the Department of Justice initiate appropriate action.

The OFCCP does not have to limit itself to a specific complaint; it has authority to probe *all* aspects of any employment practices that are suspected of being discriminatory. Unlike the EEOC, the OFCCP need not defer to local agencies.

Local Agencies

The mandates of state, city, and county agencies vary widely and cannot be adequately covered here. Frequently these agencies hold jurisdiction over a wide range of organizations, including those with fewer than 15 employees. Because of the many regional differences, each manager should take the time to become familiar with the local agencies whose jurisdiction is relevant to his or her organization.

It is important to differentiate the effect of Equal Employment Opportunity from that of Affirmative Action. Affirmative Action places the force of law behind a social philosophy that seeks elimination of past and present discrimination through the placement, promotion or other accelerated advancement of protected classes.

Equal Employment Opportunity legislation, on the other hand, puts the force of the law behind what are quite simply good personnel practices. Basically, E.E.O. informs us that, if performance appraisal scores or ratings are used in whole or in part for any personnel decisions including selection, promotion, demotion, termination, special assignment, training, transfer, or related decisions the appraisal system must be *reliable* and *valid*.

The astute reader will have already taken note of the term "and related decisions." This "umbrella clause" warns us that virtually *any* personnel decision that significantly affects an employee can lead to a legitimate challenge of the system's reliability and validity.

RELIABILITY

It is important to recognize that the performance appraisal system is a measurement device, like rulers, thermometers, weight scales and clocks are measurement devices. The term "reliability" refers simply to consistency in measurement.

When a wristwatch or alarm clock becomes erratic, the problem is generally noticed quickly—especially if we oversleep or arrive late to an important appointment. Our mechanism for measuring time has become *unreliable,* and we either replace it or get it repaired.

Reliability in the context of performance appraisal is more complex (and unfortunately the mechanisms designed to measure it are more difficult to repair). In practical terms, reliability implies the following:

Consistency Within a Given Rater

The time of day, day of week, or mood of the evaluator should have little impact on an employee's rating. For example, the rating given by a rater on a Monday morning should be very close to the rating given by the same rater on Thursday afternoon. If raters evaluate their employees twice in a five or ten-day period, there should not be wide variation in the ratings given to the same person on the two occasions. If there are, the performance appraisal system is probably not reliable. An unreliable rating system frequently tells us more about how the rater is feeling than about the performance of the person being rated.

Consistency Between Raters

All raters should be applying the rating form in the same fashion. If two raters are equally familiar with ten employees, and the raters each evaluate the ten employees, there should be general similarity between their ratings. If there is little or no similarity, then the rating form is unreliable. An actual example of poor inter-rater reliability is described later in this chapter. The problem is particularly likely to appear if raters must supply their own definitions and standards to the criteria on the appraisal form.

Since it is increasingly common for subordinates to split reporting responsibility among two or more supervisors, the problem of inter-rater reliability is significant for many organizations.

Freedom from Bias

A good rating form will make it difficult to allow a rater's personal biases to influence the ratings. The more subjective the rating criteria, the easier it is for the raters' biases to enter into his evaluation. Consider, for example, a criterion such as "Neatness of Appearance." In the absence of descriptive standards, the rater's personal biases (both conscious and subconscious) will run free.

To summarize, confidence in the reliability of our performance appraisal system requires assurance of consistency within raters over time, consistency between raters monitoring similar performance, and effective means to control personal bias.

VALIDITY

Validity refers to the accuracy of the ratings given by the raters, and focuses on the degree to which the performance appraisal reflects actual job performance. If an appraisal system is valid, the employees who receive high performance ratings are in fact the best performers and those employees who receive the lowest ratings are actually the poorest performers. Unfortunately, in many organizations everyone receives an above-average or outstanding rating, resulting in an invalid appraisal system (or an "automatic" longevity system).

More specifically, validity refers to three factors in performance appraisal:

The Rating Criteria are Job-Related

This means that the criteria used to evaluate performance are directly related to the job of the person being evaluated. Thus far most enforcement attention has been focused on selection criteria, but enforcement agencies are increasingly looking at appraisal criteria as well.

Until a few years ago a police department required that prospective officers be at least 6'2" tall. On the one hand, it might seem reasonable that a police officer be physically imposing. On the other hand, such a requirement systematically discriminates against certain population classes (e.g., women, Spanish surname, Asian American). Such criteria are not considered discriminatory, however, if they can be shown to be job related. The police agency in question was unable to show job relatedness, and had to drop the height requirement. Their case may have been weakened by another aspect of that requirement: if the candidate possessed a college degree, the height requirement was reduced to 6'1". Common sense dictates that employees be evaluated for the work they are performing. There must be different criteria for the different jobs or job families in the organization. Should a secretary be evaluated on the same rating form as a police officer? The answer of course is no. Yet most organizations have one form with identical criteria for evaluating all of their employees. In one large organization, the authors found nearly 900 job titles—from "truck driver" to "counselor"—covered by a single appraisal form.

There may be a few criteria applicable to all employees, but the majority of the criteria must be job-specific if they are to be meaningful.

The Criteria Include all Important Job Factors

One of the essential functions of the appraisal form is to communicate to the employees those factors on which their performance will be rated. If an employee receives "good" ratings on all of the criteria, then the employee is seen by his boss as a "good" employee, and "good" employees will receive "good" ratings on the criteria. If, however, these correlations do not hold, then the rating criteria may not represent the key aspects of the job. If it is possible for an employee to achieve a rating of "good" on all of the criteria and at the same time be performing at an unsatisfactory level, then one or more important criteria have been omitted.

For example, if our rating criteria include only the following four job factors, then the message to employees is that these four factors are the most important aspects of their jobs:

Criterion 1—Willingness to help co-workers

Criterion 2—Oral communication skills

Criterion 3—Meets deadlines

Criterion 4—Attendance

If it is possible for one to receive a high rating on these four criteria and still be a poor performer, then something must be missing. Take, for instance, a clerk typist whose job is rated by the above criteria. It is quite possible that he could rate high on willingness to help, oral communications, meeting deadlines, and attendance and yet be a poor performer. Why? Because the evaluation does not include criteria for speed of typing, errors per page, or other important aspects of the typist's job.

In the case of employees who are in regular contact with consumers of the organization's goods and services, it is usually important for the client's needs to be considered in selecting appraisal criteria.

For example, advertisements for major United States airlines periodically highlight their reservation agents' friendliness and concern to get the best schedule at the best price for the airline's passengers. Yet, one major airline evaluates its agents exclusively on the following five factors:

1. Calls handled per hour
2. Revenue (dollar value of bookings per hour)
3. Sales factor (a weighted indicator based on a sales/calls ratio)

4. Number of tickets mailed (the lowest cost method of handling)
5. Number of rental cars booked

Note that the criteria are all based upon volume. There is precious little incentive for the agent to seek out the lowest fare for the client.

There is no requirement that the airline live up to its implied promise of course, but the reality must be confusing to the rooky reservation agent who has seen and believed the public image. The reservation agent may then live up to the advertising myth only at some risks to his/her airline career. Meanwhile those of us who fly frequently gaze wistfully at the advertisements and endure the reality.

The Criteria Reflect Actual Differences in Performance

The ratings given by raters should clearly differentiate different levels of employee performance. It makes no sense for all performers to receive the same or even approximately the same rating regardless of performance. Poor performers should receive below standard ratings, employees meeting job standards should receive standard ratings, and above standard performers should receive above standard ratings. Each rating criterion must include definitions of "above standard performance," "performance that meets job standards" and 'below standard performance." These definitions insure at least some uniformity of application by raters.

CHECKING FOR RATER BIAS

Appraisal systems should be neutral when it comes to race, sex, age, marital status, etc.; however, *raters* may still have biases. Some of the more common problems are described in "Rater Errors."

There are a number of E.E.O. questions raised concerning reliability and validity, and most organizations can be required to provide answers. Typical questions are:

Are minorities consistently rated lower (or higher) than whites?

Are women consistently rated lower (or higher) than men?

Are older employeees consistently rated lower (or higher) than younger employees?

Is any one job classification consistently rated lower (or higher) than another classification?

Needless to say, your organization should keep ahead of the game by gathering statistics for internal use—not just in order to anticipate an EEO audit, but to improve the quality of managerial practices.

Perhaps the best technique is to study the actual ratings given to employees, via the following steps:

Step 1. For each employee rated, compute an overall rating. This can be computed by adding all the ratings given to an employee over the year and dividing the number of non-zero ratings given. Note that numerical ratings can be assigned for purposes of analysis, even if your appraisal form does not quantify ratings.

For example, a form might have the following performance levels: Outstanding, Exceeds Requirements, Meets Requirements, Needs Improvement, Unsatisfactory, Not Applicable/No Opportunity to Observe. For analysis, one simply assigns a number value to the ratings, e.g.,:

Outstanding	= 5
Exceeds Requirements	= 4
Meets Requirements	= 3
Needs Improvement	= 2
Unsatisfactory	= 1
Not Applicable/No Opportunity to Observe	= 0

Step 2. Group employees into subgroups using the following E.E.O.C. classifications:

A. Racial minorities
B. Women
C. Persons over 40 years of age
D. Handicapped persons
E. White males under 40 years of age

Step 3. For each group listed in Step 2, compute the average ratings received by members of that group. For example, assume that a small company employs ten women. The average ratings for each of the ten women computed in Step 1 are: 1.87, 2.34, 2.78, 3.12, 3.36, 3.97, 3.99, 4.23, 4.56. Total the ten ratings and divide by ten. The average rating received by women employees is 3.41. Repeat this process for all the subgroups listed in Step 2.

Step 4. Present the results as in Table 4.1 below and compare the ratings received by the various groups.

Table 4.1. Average ratings received by different subgroups

Subgroups	Average Rating
Women	3.11
Minorities	3.40
Persons over 40	3.42
Handicapped persons	3.42
White males under 40	3.43

The figures in Table 4.1 indicate that there may be discrimination in that women receive lower performance ratings. The reader should note that there are statistical tests of significance that can be applied to the data to see whether there is actually a significant difference.

Averages should also be gathered for the nine job categories that all organizations use in completing E.E.O. reports: officials/managers, professionals, technicians, sales workers, operatives, office/clerical, craft workers, service workers, laborers. Obviously, small organizations may not have employees in every category. Consider the following average ratings for one organization:

Table 4.2. Average ratings received by E.E.O. job categories

Job Categories	Average Rating
Officials/Managers	4.46
Professionals	4.36
Technicians	3.44
Sales Workers	3.30
Office/Clerical	3.86
Craft Workers	3.21
Service Workers	3.44
Operatives	2.68
Laborers	2.30

Notice that as we go from upper level jobs to lower level jobs, there is a distinct tendency for the average rating to decrease. These ratings may imply systematic bias on the basis of job level. There is probably no actual difference in ability to perform between the various levels, since employees *should be evaluated on criteria and standards related to their jobs* (validity). There is no reason why employees' ratings should be increasingly higher with increasingly demanding jobs, thus there is no a priori reason to assume that the average service/maintenance employee performs less adequately *at that job* than the average official/administrator performs at his/her job.

Does a markedly higher or lower subgroup rating indicate certain discrimination? The answer is usually yes, but it may be no. For example, an organization may have recently initiated a vigorous affirmative action program, with the result that many women and minorities are essentially trainees. This could lead to lower ratings for women and minorities which reflect their relative inexperience in their positions.

While information of the kind presented in Tables 4.1 and 4.2 does not give definitive indication of discrimination, it does indicate where one should *look* for potential discrimination. In the example in Table 4.1, the organization should investigate further why women are receiving lower ratings, while in Table 4.2, investigation should focus on why employees in lower prestige positions are receiving lower ratings. If the problem stems from rater bias, this indicates a need for reviewing the appraisal system, and possibly for training raters.

For larger organizations, a matrix of average ratings can easily be constructed. Table 4.3 presents one possible matrix.

Table 4.3. Average ratings received by subgroups and by job categories

Job Categories	Subgroups				
	Women	Minorities	Persons over 40	Handicapped	White Males under 40
Officials/Administrators					
Professionals					
Technicians					
Sales Workers					
Office/Clerical					
Craft Workers					
Service Workers					
Operatives					
Laborers					

Any organization of 100 employees or more should find the matrix useful in discerning anomalies in employee average performance ratings.

COMMON RATER ERRORS

Even after we have developed a reliable and valid performance appraisal system, the job is only partially complete. We must turn our attention to the users and train them in both the mechanics of the system and in rater errors.

Imagine three baseball umpires talking to one another prior to a game and discussing their philosophies of umpiring. Umpire #1: "Sometimes the pitcher throws strikes and sometimes he throws balls, but I call them as I see them." Umpire #2: "Sometimes the pitcher throws strikes and sometimes he throws balls, but I call them as they are." Umpire #3: "Yeah, sometimes the pitcher throws strikes and sometimes he throws balls, but they are not anything until I call them."

That conversation may confirm the suspicions of the avid baseball fan, but more importantly it reflects a common problem in evaluation of human performance: differing values of those doing the rating. Imagine the pitcher as a subordinate and the three umpires as supervisors for whom the pitcher works over a period of time. Even though his level of performance remains stable, the hapless subordinate might receive three considerably different performance ratings. If the performance is consistent and yet the evaluations are not, this is an example of rater error.

By rater error we mean any attitude, response, tendency, or inconsistency within the rater which interferes with accurate performance ratings. The rater may or may not be aware of making any errors. He or she may attribute the inconsistencies in ratings to inconsistency in the performance of the ratee, and not recognize them as inconsistencies in the ratings themselves. Often simply alerting raters to the fact that errors in rating can occur and pointing out some fairly simple techniques for avoiding them will markedly reduce their occurrence.

Below are actual ratings given to a single worker by two different supervisors:

Supervisor #1		*Supervisor #2*
Unfavorable to people	—	Is open, honest, straight-forward
High and mighty with superior attitude	—	Extremely self-confident and knowledgeable
Company owes	—	Needs reciprocal respect and common courtesy
Hard to talk to, gets easily "heated"	—	Well informed, likes to debate and brainstorm
		Wants to understand others' rationale
Tries to solve problems without help	—	Shows initiative
Knows less than he thinks	—	Knows more than given credit for
Must be asked twice before anything gets done	—	Has large volume of work and different priorities than those requesting

Figure 4.1 Ratings given one employee by independent raters

Needless to say, the employee who received these ratings was confused and angry. Each supervisor thought the other to be demented, and the personnel department concluded that both were correct in their assessment of the other.

Though the magnitude of differences is not usually this great, the problem of differential rating is not at all rare.

Look at the two sets of ratings again. Remember that these ratings are for one person, given by two different supervisors observing essentially the same activities. Clearly at least one of these ratings is completely in error.

This is an example of inconsistency between raters. It is possible that both raters are biased toward this employee—one in a positive direction and the other in a negative direction. Although we can't tell from the ratings which is "most" correct, we can say unequivocally that this firms's evaluation system is both a waste of time and a legal landmine. The two raters obviously have no standards by which to judge performance. How useful is the feedback on these ratings going to be to the employee?

The system is a legal landmine because we have hard copy evidence that it is *neither* reliable nor valid.

Let us look at the most common rater errors, and then at ways to reduce their severity. It cannot be over-emphasized that rater errors *will* occur in any performance system. In practical terms, it is impossible to eliminate rater errors, but it is imperative they be controlled.

Most Common Rater Errors

Halo Effect

This is the tendency to rate a person who is outstandingly good on one factor high on all other factors. One factor unduly influences the other ratings.

Horns Effect

This is the opposite side of the Halo Effect—a tendency to rate a person who is very poor on one factor low on all other factors.

Central Tendency

As its name suggests, this error is the tendency of raters to avoid both high and low extremes, lumping all ratings in the middle category.

Positive Leniency

This occurs when the rater gives all high ratings or a disproportionate number of high ratings.

Negative Leniency

When the rater gives all low ratings or a disproportionate number of low ratings, the rater may be erring in the direction of negative leniency.

Similar-to-Me

Many raters have a tendency to give persons similar to them higher ratings on the basis of biographical backgrounds, attitudes, etc.

Contrast Effect

This is the tendency of raters to evaluate persons relative to each other, rather than on the basis of the performance evaluation criteria.

Now let us look more closely at the rater errors and at ways to reduce them.

HALO AND HORNS EFFECT

We have seen that the Halo (Horns) effect is the tendency to generalize from one specific employee trait or behavior to other employee characteristics. One very positive trait may create a "halo" blinding the rater to shortcomings in the person being rated. The halo effect is occurring, for instance, when a person who has recently solved an important departmental problem receives very high ratings on every factor because of the recent success in problem solving.

In the horns effect, one very obvious weakness may blind the rater to strengths in the person being rated. In effect, these errors result in raters giving twenty ratings for one factor, rather than rating on twenty different factors.

Halo errors often occur when the rater is rating employees who have markedly pleasant or unpleasant personality characteristics. If a person is considerate and friendly—perhaps volunteers frequently for special assignments—the performance rating in unrelated aspects of performance may be unduly influenced. Obviously the reverse will tend to be true for the surly, uncooperative employee. A more subtle aspect of the Halo (Horns) effect results when the rater does not maintain a performance diary. We tend to remember unusual events; typical actions fade into oblivion. As my boss, you can surely recall the time I dropped a handful of paperclips into the copying machine, causing a 400 dollar repair bill. You can certainly remember the day I backed the forklift off the edge of the loading dock. You may even remember the time I noted errors in shipping documents and saved the organization several thousand dollars in late delivery penalties. As important as these events are, they are probably not typical of my overall performance. Yet they will almost certainly influence aspects of my evaluation in ways far beyond their true significance, unless we have performance standards *and* my boss is very careful in the rating process.

Reducing the Halo and Horns Effect

Ask yourself if the person being rated has done anything outstandingly good or bad in the past few months. If the answer is yes, be extra careful in your ratings.

Ask yourself if the person being rated has a very pleasant or unpleasant personality. Again, if the answer is yes, be extra careful in your ratings.

Be thoroughly familiar with all the rating criteria. Know how the criteria differ from each other and why they are important for the job being rated.

Rate one criterion at a time. For example, rate all persons being rated one by one on the first criterion. Then rate on the second criterion. If possible, cover your ratings for the preceding criteria to reduce their influence on you.

Use behaviorally based performance evaluation criteria.

CENTRAL TENDENCY AND LENIENCY

The central tendency error occurs when the rater hesitates to use the ends of the performance evaluation scale. This results in most of the ratings falling in the middle of the scale, often with 90 percent or even 100 percent of the ratings in the middle and no ratings at either end of the scale.

Positive and negative leniency refers to the rater's frame of reference used in rating. Positive leniency is the tendency to be overly easy in the ratings, thereby giving too many high ratings. Negative leniency refers to the tendency to be overly severe in rating and to give too many low ratings. Both "easy" and "hard" raters have a negative impact on the total performance evaluation system, by making the evaluation process more a function of the rater's standards than of actual employee performance.

Clusters of high, average or low ratings are not *necessarily* rating errors. After all, some employees or even units are truly outstanding in most aspects of their performance. But let us face it; they are few and far between. Consider an employee rated on 20 performance criteria:

Table 4.4. Example of leniency error

Rating Values: Outstanding = 5, Exceeds Expectations = 4, Meets Expectations = 3, Needs Improvement = 2, Unsatisfactory = 1

Criterion	*Rating*
1. Oral Communication	5
2. Written Communication	5
3. Decision Making	5
4. Delegating Authority	5
5. Leadership	4
6. Organizing, Coordinating	5
7. Meeting Deadlines and Commitments	5
8. Flexibility and Adaptability	5
9. Creativity	5
10. Public Contact	5
11. Job Knowledge	5
12. Setting and Meeting Goals and Objectives	5
13. Planning	5
14. Cooperation and Participation	5
15. Interpersonal Skills	4
16. Integrity	5
17. Budgeting Skills	5
18. Employee Development	4
19. Initiative	5
20. Problem Solving	5

How likely it is that this person is truly outstanding on 17 out of 20 criteria? Note that many of the criteria are unrelated, calling for a wide range of abilities. Although it is possible that an employee might be outstanding in all facets of a job, it is rather unusual. When ratings are tightly clustered, the burden of proof must fall on the rater. This requirement is not as weighty as it may appear. If a supervisor has set good performance criteria and standards, kept performance notes and done a conscientious job of rating, he or she can easily convince an independent observer of the rating's accuracy. (Incidentally, if the reader knows an employee as good as our example, please refer him or her to us. We need a ghost writer for our next book.)

Let us examine some of the motivations behind erroneous groupings of performance ratings. The person who consistently rates employees higher than they deserve may be somewhat insecure in his or her own job. It is also possible that the rater has a strong need to be liked by employees, and few things make a performance review session more pleasant than delivering high ratings.

The supervisor who tends to rate employees in a narrow range at the middle of the scale may literally not know what the employees are doing. A rating of "meets expectations," "average," or "meets standards" may be a "safe" rating. Occasionally, we have seen the performance system itself encourage central tendency by requiring that all ratings above or below average be supported with essay type information. In such a case, many supervisors will give "average" ratings to avoid having to explain ratings. The lesson here, of course, is that if ratings are to be supported at all, they should be supported no matter what the rating. Requiring documentation of high and low ratings exclusively will virtually guarantee system-wide central tendency.

The supervisor who tends to give low ratings may justify the act to self and others by saying that he or she has very high standards, or wants to challenge employees to do their best. In theory, of course, there is nothing wrong with having high standards or with challenging people to do their best, as long as the challenge is reasonable and attainable. However, by adopting unusually rigorous standards, the supervisor is in effect punishing employees, since he rates them lower than another supervisor would for similar performance. The time for challenging employees to do their best is at the point when standards and expectations are being defined—not at appraisal time. Once standards have been set for a job category, it is the duty of the rater to apply them as defined, rather than substituting his or her own (and perhaps undefined) expectations.

Reducing Central Tendency and Leniency Errors

When you give an employee an "average" rating, ask yourself whether you are rating on the basis of actual performance, or whether you really *don't know* how well this person is performing.

After rating an employee or employees, count the number of ratings in each category. If you find 75 percent or more of the ratings for any person or group of people in the same category, ask yourself why. Think carefully about your ratings, then rate the person once again. If you have the same results after a second rating, it is likely to be a good rating. But it is important to ask the question.

Provide raters with feedback on how their own ratings compared to other raters. It is usually an easy task to aggregate ratings on a departmental basis. For comparison purposes, a distribution of average ratings for similar units can then be prepared and given to individual supervisors. For example, a chart can be prepared as follows:

Table 4.5. Average unit rating

	Units			
Criteria	Engineering	Sales	Steno/Typing	R & D
Initiative	4.30	4.60	4.52	4.35
Monitoring	4.62	4.21	4.44	4.00
Oral Communication	4.11	4.33	4.40	4.10

It is useful for the rater to know how he or she compares with other raters in the same organization. These data also will aid personnel people in determining whether the system is being used fairly.

Provide raters with the option of checking the following statements:

a. This criterion is not applicable.
b. I have not had an opportunity to observe behavior related to this criterion.

If raters are required to rate on every criterion, they will tend to do so even when information is lacking. Performance assessment is too critical to allow guessing games.

Use behaviorally based performance evaluation criteria.

SIMILAR-TO-ME ERROR

The "similar-to-me" error refers to the tendency to give preferential ratings to persons who are similar to us in attitudes, education, income, hobby interests, etc. An apocryphal story may serve to illustrate: A want ad appeared in the New Haven, Connecticut newspaper, looking for a "Yale graduate or equivalent." In the next day's mail came a letter from Cambridge, Massachusetts. The letter said, in part, "Please clarify what you mean by 'Yale graduate or equivalent.' Do you want two Princeton graduates or one Harvard graduate part-time?"

That story highlights what research has shown and what most people suspect anyway: raters tend to favor those subordinates similar to themselves. This error becomes increasingly important as the similarities between the rater and the ratee become more pronounced. It is also likely that when *differences* between manager and subordinate are pronounced, a reverse effect to "similar-to-me" may occur.

Raters who are blatantly prejudiced can generally be quickly identified and dealt with accordingly, but the more subtle forms of similar-to-me error are difficult to combat. The "old boy network" is one example of the similar-to-me phenomenon.

The more similarities between the rater and the ratee, the more likely it is that the rater will commit a similar-to-me error. What are the similarities that may cause problems? Name your poison. . . . From very visible similarities like age, race, or sex, to educational background, rural versus city childhood, manner of speech and dress, hobbies, religion, etc.

Similar-to-me can be especially deadly in the evaluation of employees in EEO protected classes. Over the past four to five years, several hundreds of millions of dollars have been spent in out-of-court settlements against employers and supervisors who did not guard against this pervasive error. If we find that we are rating in terms of a stereotype, such as "women tend to be . . . ," or, "Asian-Americans usually are . . . ," then we are probably making the similar-to-me error.

CONTRAST EFFECT

The Contrast Effect error takes a number of different forms. It occurs when employees are rated relative to other employees; rather than to performance standards, and, ratings reflect the supervisor's attitude toward a trait. Take the following example: on a scale of one to ten, where one is low, rate a Chevrolet in terms of cost. Now think of a Mercedes Benz and rate the Mercedes on a scale of one to ten. Now go back and re-rate the Chevrolet. If you are tempted to give the Chevrolet a lower rating, you have made a contrast effect error. Note that the dollar cost of the Chevrolet is fixed, but its value tended to seem lower when compared to the Mercedes Benz.

Let us apply the Contrast Effect error to a job situation. You are evaluating employees A, B, and C on the criterion "Report Writing." Employee A gets reports in on time, but they need occasional correction and reworking. You assign Employee A a rating of "Meets Standards for 'Report Writing' ." You then turn to Employee B. Employee B usually has reports in early, and they rarely need correction or reworking. The quality of Employee B's reports has also been favorably noted by your boss. Employee B receives a rating of "Outstanding." Now you evaluate Employee C, who has just completed her first year at the present position. By common consensus, she is the best report writer in the eastern half of the state. Employee C's reports are models of clarity and completeness, yet brief and to the point. She receives a truly deserved "Outstanding" rating. Now wait a minute! Employee C is noticeably better than Employee B, so now you decide to lower Employee B's ratings one step, to "Exceeds Expectations," still a very favorable rating. But wait another minute! Employee B is AT LEAST two performance levels above Employee A, so Employee A's initial rating of "Meets Standards" now becomes "Needs Improvement"!!! An unusual example? Unfortunately not.

Note that the operations above took place in your head, not in the actual behavior of employee A, B, or C. The changes in the ratings would imply to Employee A that his/her performance has changed. If Employee A used to get a "Satisfactory" rating but now "Needs Improvement" simply because Employee C has joined the crew and thrown the rating scale off, there is a problem. You have committed the common but unforgivable error of applying a comparative, or flexible, standard. A flexible standard is a contradiction in terms. Employees should be evaluated against standards, rather than against other employees. The truly exceptional employee can be acknowledged by the addition of comments attached to the appraisal form. The "Satisfactory" employee should not be punished through comparison to an exceptional employee.

Reducing Similar-to-Me and Contrast Effect Errors

Try to avoid cataloging people. Ask yourself if you are rating a particular employee or if you are really rating the employee on the basis of a stereotype—rating of a whole class of people.

Resist the urge to return to other employees whom you have already rated and to change their ratings because you have just given a very high or very low rating and now have changed your "standard."

Study the ratings you have given to determine whether you are giving high ratings to employees who are very similar to you. *You* know the employees who are most similar and least similar to you in attitudes, etc. It might be helpful to prepare a table showing the ratings. If it appears that employees similar to you have systematically higher ratings and the employees most unlike you have systematically lower ratings, go back and re-evaluate everyone.

Use behaviorally-based performance evaluation criteria.

CHAPTER

5

The Formal Review Session

Though performance appraisal systems can serve a wide variety of purposes, their potential can only be achieved when the employee receives the information he needs to improve his performance.

It is not enough for management to work on developing better task descriptions, more appropriate forms, or more objective standards for rating. These are important steps toward a better performance evaluation, for ultimately they lead to a more informed evaluation. But what about the responsibility for communicating that information to the employee? Unless the contents are shared with the employee, filling out forms is an altogether ritualistic and useless procedure. Some organizations require supervisors to faithfully complete evaluation forms, only to mechanically file them away afterwards. This practice makes performance appraisal a charade: management pats itself on the back for having done its duty, but the employee learns nothing about his performance on the job. Other organizations make the effort to communicate the evaluation results to the employee, but do so in a manner which undermines the evaluation—sometimes so thoroughly that the employee wonders why management bothers to engage in performance evaluation in the first place. The supervisor who prefaces a performance evaluation with, "Well, Hal, it's time we got the semi-yearly nonsense out of the way" has, in effect, discounted all that is to follow and ensured that in fact very little will follow.

Happily, such organizations and supervisors are the exception and not the rule. The performance appraisal process rests on the assumption that management will devote as much careful preparation to communicating information as it will devote to acquiring that information. The performance appraisal interview (PAI) is a formal structure designed to provide an employee with information on his/her job performance on an annual or a semi-annual basis. When management is inadequately prepared for the PAI, many months of effort are placed in jeopardy. Recognizing how crucial it is that the interview be much more than a casual conversation, this chapter focuses on the interview itself, particularly on those aspects of the interview which are often neglected or even ignored.

FEAR OF APPRAISAL

One aspect of appraisal that frequently is not considered, is the fear that many people have about being evaluated. Even the best appraisal system cannot entirely quell that fear.

The employee is frequently not the only fearful party; many supervisors also fear the PAI, though for somewhat different reasons. Supervisors frequently feel unsure about what is supposed to be communicated in the PAI, and mistakenly assume that only negative aspects of performance should be the focal point. Nothing could be further from the truth, since good performance deserves recognition and should be praised. Most appraisal interviews will contain some elements of criticism. Yet the PAI is almost never entirely negative, for it is the rare employee who does nothing right! Even when critical comments are necessary, there is no reason that the PAI should not be a positive, even pleasant, experience for both employee and supervisor.

The objective of the PAI is communication and it is important that the supervisor do all he can in advance to see that the important issues are communicated. This requires at least a modest amount of thought in advance of the formal session, so that the supervisor knows what he intends to communicate as well as how he is going to communicate it. For purposes of planning, the session can be conceived as having six parts:

 I. Interview preparation
 II. Interview initiation
 III. Interview structuring
 IV. Interview communication
 V. Interview planning
 VI. Interview closing

I. INTERVIEW PREPARATION

Interview preparation refers to the "homework" the supervisor must do before the review session. This "homework" includes reviewing the performance criteria and standards, studying the individual employee's performance record, assessing the employee's performance on key objectives, considering the employee's career development, and completing the rating form. If self evaluation is to be part of the PAI, the employee should, of course, be provided with a copy of the rating form. In any event, the employee should be reminded a day or two in advance that the review session is pending. In scheduling the interviews, ample time should be reserved for the review session, so that neither party feels rushed.

II. INTERVIEW INITIATION

Interview initiation deals with those verbal and nonverbal interactions that occur during the first few minutes (even the first few seconds) of an appraisal interview—the moment of truth, when the employee enters the inner sanctum. If the interview is to be productive, it is absolutely crucial to put the employee at ease from the moment he walks in the doors. One of the most effective ways to accomplish this is to immediately tell the employee the purpose of the review session; namely, it is a *joint* discussion of how things are going on the job. Potential anxiety can also be substantially reduced by telling each employee that review sessions are conducted with all employees on an annual or semi-annual basis. Much more will be said about these early moments of the interview when we discuss interview communication.

III. INTERVIEW STRUCTURING

The supervisor should let the employee know well in advance how the interview will be structured. Don't assume that the employee already understands the nature of your performance appraisal system and the performance appraisal process. There are at least three specific areas about which the employee should be informed before the interview:

1. The goals and uses of performance appraisal in your personnel system: i.e., why appraisals are conducted and which types of personnel decisions are affected by performance ratings.

2. The specific objectives of the review session. Usually the objectives will include one or more of the following:
   —specific feedback on performance;
   —discussion of general issues or concerns about job performance;
   —discussion of opportunities for growth or improvement;
   —formation of an employee development plan.

3. The outline of the review session and the events that will occur during the session. This third item is nothing more than an agenda. While most people would agree that a meeting needs an agenda, many have not yet recognized that the appraisal interview is in fact a meeting, though limited to two people.

It is very important that these areas be discussed with *each* employee to be interviewed. Don't rely on a memo or general announcement. Inform the employee of the time periods under consideration. For example, you might be reviewing performance for the last six months and setting performance objectives for the next six months. Specify the extent to which the session is to involve mutual planning. Define your expectations for the meeting and for the flow of events. If your intent is to discuss each rating and solicit comments from the employee as you go, say so. If you prefer to go over all the ratings and hold discussion until afterwards, say so. If you plan to use self-evaluation, inform the employee whether his self-evaluation will be discussed at the beginning, throughout, or toward the end of the interview. Many supervisors have found that it is helpful to make an outline of the points they wish to cover during the session, and to provide the employee with an agenda listing the sequence of events.

A useful motto for the appraisal interview (indeed for the entire appraisal process) should be: "no surprises." Communication is most complete in a surprise-free atmosphere. Any time a "bomb" is dropped, communication invariably suffers.

IV. INTERVIEW COMMUNICATION

The PAI *is* communication, of course, but the quality of communication can vary greatly. There are specific skills related to good communication practice, and we will consider them in some detail here.

VERBAL COMMUNICATION

Most people fancy themselves to be good communicators. Yet when we observe those we work with, we see a very wide range of communicative abilities. It is instructive (and occasionally entertaining) to watch both extremes, the very good and the very poor communicators. You may wish to conduct your own *ad hoc* communication study by singling out both good and poor communicators in your organization. If you look more closely at what distinguishes these two groups, we'd be willing to wager that you'll see the good communicators are experts at the following fundamental communication skills: attending, facilitating, paraphrasing, clarifying, and feeding back.

Each of the five skills are expressed in visible actions, which could number in the hundreds for each skill. It is not our intent to provide a comprehensive list of communication behavior, but definitions of the skills and some behaviors frequently associated with each are considered in the context of the PAI. The reader can probably provide other examples from experience.

Attending

This skill refers to behaviors that show the employee that you are listening to what he or she is saying. Some things you can do to show that you are attending include:

1. Maintain eye contact (not a stare, of course). Look directly at the employee when you are speaking and when you are listening.
2. Maintain a relaxed posture. This will convey to the employee that you are comfortable.

3. Make verbal statements that "follow" what the employee has said, i.e., your statement should be consistent with the topic that s/he is discussing.
4. Try not to interrupt the employee.
5. Throw the ball to the employee and ask how s/he feels things are going on the job. Then listen.

Facilitating

This skill includes behaviors designed to make communication flow more smoothly. By facilitating, the supervisor (or rater) is inviting the employee to say more about a particular topic, to give more specific examples, and so on. Some things you can do to facilitate:

1. Make specific verbal invitations that encourage the employee to state a position or to explore further a stated position. Some facilitating statements or expressions might be: "Can you say more?" "Would you elaborate?" "I'd like to hear more about that." "Can you give me an example?" "Can you give me more detail?" "Do you see any problems we should discuss?" "Do you have any suggestions for improving the way we are operating?"
2. Make specific nonverbal invitations to encourage the employee to talk, such as: Head nods, eye contact, leaning forward, narrowing physical distance (moving closer together).

It is inappropriate to argue or state strongly your own position at this time. Doing so will disrupt, if not cripple, the communication process. If the employee expresses some concerns with which you agree or disagree, it's a good idea to take notes during the interview so that you will be sure to return to those points later in the interview.

Paraphrasing

This communication skill involves the brief restatement by the supervisor (or rater) of some prior verbal communication made by the employee. The restatement communicates the same meaning in fewer words. By paraphrasing you are accomplishing at least two things:

1. The employee is assured that you are following the conversation (attending) in terms of thoughts and feelings.
2. The employee's thoughts are condensed or presented in a more concise way. You are providing feedback to assure that communication with understanding is taking place.

You should attempt to paraphrase every major point made by your subordinate. This practice will make you a more effective communicator.

Clarifying

During the performance review session it is likely that the employee will express some incomplete thoughts, will have difficulty expressing some thoughts, will say things you don't understand, or will simply "lose" you. Clarifying behaviors are specific verbal cues on the supervisor's part that admit a lack of understanding about employee communications. Some examples of clarifying statements and questions are: "I'm confused." "Can you give me an example?" "Can you restate that?" "I lost you there." "I need more information about that."

It is important to note that the emphasis here is upon "I" statements as opposed to "you" statements. Saying "I'm confused or "I'm not sure I understand" has a far more positive effect on the employee being evaluated than "you're confusing me" or "you're not being clear." The first two quotes are invitations, whereas the last two statements are accusations.

Feeding Back

Up to this point in the review session, the communication focus has been on encouraging the employee to talk while the supervisor (or rater) concentrates on attending to the employee through facilitating, paraphrasing, and asking for clarification. Feeding back, however, also occurs throughout the interview. Feeding back includes statements made by the supervisor which relate to the employees performance during the review period. In providing feedback, the supervisor (rater) should:

1. Describe employee behavior. Feedback should refer to specific behaviors and not employee attitudes. Behavior can be described in definite terms by a supervisor (rater). It is also easier for an employee to change a specific behavior than to change an attitude.
2. Identify specific critical incidents. Indicate what happened, when it happened, where it happened, and the outcome of the incident. Also provide the employee with information about how often the behavior has been observed.
3. Address previously agreed-upon goals. Focus your feedback on those aspects of job performance where goals have been established.
4. Focus on important job dimensions. Don't deal with minor infractions of little significance. The time to discuss those problems is when they occur—discuss them at that time, then forget them.
5. Give recognition for desirable performance which you would like to see continued. The importance of this point cannot be overstated.
6. Reiterate the previously established performance criteria and standards.
7. Check and clarify to insure clear communication. Good feedback calls for a mutual exchange to be sure that communication has been understood.

Learning to be a good communicator is much like learning to be a good swimmer or cyclist—the skills must be consciously practiced until they become almost reflex. No textbook or manual can turn a novice into an expert; the expert's apparently effortless butterfly stroke is based on hour after hour of concentrated practice. The same is true of communicating; workshops and seminars can help sharpen communication skills, but they will never become second nature without constant, conscious practice. Paraphrasing and feeding back may seem mechanical at first, but they become "natural" in time.

NONVERBAL COMMUNICATION

Interview communication involves more than just words. Behavioral scientists have estimated that as much as seventy percent of the meaning of a communication derives from the nonverbal aspects of the interchange and as little as thirty percent from the words used. To be insensitive to setting, posture or "body language," and verbal inflection is to enter the PAI with blinders on. To ignore so large a portion of the communicated message is to deny responsibility for the content of the total message communicated. The concerned manager should prepare himself for the PAI by developing an awareness of how nonverbal messages affect communication. He should become aware of the costs of ignoring the nonverbal elements of the interview, elements we now consider in detail. The first is the environment or interview setting.

SETTING

Case #1

Mrs. Smith busily scurries around the house, nervously dusting obscure corners, rearranging her dried flowers for the third time, and making minor adjustments in the placement of ashtrays. This obsessive and uncharacteristic behavior becomes readily understandable once we know that her always tidy and sometimes subtly critical mother-in-law is coming to dinner tonight—an infrequent event.

Case #2

Private Jones is hastily reorganizing the contents of his footlocker and expresses his dissatisfaction with the task in that colorful language known only to military barracks. Having reassured himself that his never-used toiletries have been displayed in the manner prescribed by authoritative military manuals, he is now prepared for the forthcoming barracks inspection.

Case #3

David Swanson feels a great sense of release. After having visited more furniture stores than he believed existed, learned more about furniture than he ever wanted to know, and looked at sample swatches of materials until they became a collective blur in his mind, he has finally selected the furniture and upholstery for his dental office reception area.

Case #4

Bill Watts carefully places his favorite mood music record on the phonograph, re-checks the dinner wine to assure that it is properly chilled and self-consciously removes his recent copy of a "macho" men's magazine. Janice will be arriving shortly for her first meal at his bachelor apartment.

Different people, different ages, different situations. But they all have one thing in common: an awareness of the importance of a "proper setting" and the need to make a good first impression.

Every day, in hundreds of ways, each of us pays unspoken tribute to an awareness that is only sometimes conscious—the awareness that setting or staging has an impact on other persons and that we have at least some degree of power over that setting. And so, like apprentice grade Cecile B. De Milles preparing for a crowd scene in *The Ten Commandments,* or like aspiring choreographers hoping to influence the dance of life in some small way, we attend to those myriad details which impact others and, therefore, have a reciprocal consequence for us as well. To ask managers to focus on the setting of the PAI is merely to ask them to extend to one more arena that awareness which characterizes so much of their daily life.

THE INTERVIEW SETTING

Granted that we all attend to setting or staging issues in some situations, we may still wonder how we can translate this awareness into specific guidelines for settings. The translation is easier than we realize, as the following exercise illustrates. On pp. 94 and 95 are three pictures. Given the information provided in the descriptive story, which picture seems to "fit" the narrative best? As you make these associations, be aware of the cues you use. That is, why do you associate one set of information with another and on what basis? Be aware of the types of descriptive adjectives you would use to describe the setting. Do you perceive the setting to be warm, relaxed, comfortable and open, or is the setting cool, distant, tight, and constrained?

Appraisal Interview Situation A

The General Sales Manager for the Baltz Corporation gained that position by virtue of a highly successful sales record and still seeks out opportunities to get into the field and sell with the employees. The manager is not looking forward to the PAI today with a rooky sales agent.

The agent is a college graduate with an MBA from a prestigious college. When compared with other salespeople, the employee's sales record is slightly below average. Manager and agent have disagreed frequently about a variety of issues during the past six months, including marketing approaches in general, specific presentations to customers, and the method of handling competitive product intrusions into their market. The sales agent feels that the sales manager is an inept leader who lacks the skill to effectively manage sales in this increasingly sophisticated and competitive market. Like the manager, the agent is not looking forward to the PAI today, and expects to hear the same old exhortations to get out there and "give 'em hell"—an approach the agent has heard too many times before and regards as naive at best.

Appraisal Interview Situation B

The Chief Administrative Officer for Baltz Corporation is meeting with an Administrative Assistant. The two have discovered they have little in common in terms of outside office pursuits, but hold each other in reasonably high regard in terms of their day-to-day work at the office. The manager is pleased with the assistant's "take charge" approach to many administrative problems, and has made every effort to create a cooperative milieu in which both feel they are working together to solve problems. The assistant feels comfortable with the manager and expects the collaborative style which they have evolved during the nine months to characterize the PAI as well.

Appraisal Interview Situation C

In the final setting, we find an employee and manager meeting for their first PAI. Their backgrounds and business philosophies are remarkably similar. Their relationship has been remarkably smooth, and a sense of open comradeship exists between them.

The manager has been looking forward to the PAI both as a formal opportunity to give the employee some well deserved praise and as a vehicle for exploring feelings about some proposed changes in plant operation. The employee regards the manager as a relaxed yet efficient manager who has consistently demonstrated sensitivity to various plant problems which have occurred from time to time. Like the manager, the employee is looking forward to the PAI. Throughout the evaluation period, the employee has received feedback regarding performance from the manager and, for that reason, anticipates a favorable review with few unpleasant surprises.

Figure 5.1. Interview picture #1.

Figure 5.2. Interview picture #2.

Figure 5.3. Interview picture #3.

If you associated Figure 5.1 with Interview Situation "C," Figure 5.2 with Interview Situation "A" and Figure 5.3 with Interview situation "B" your response is most like that of persons who have undergone similar exercises in workshops and seminars dealing with the Appraisal Interview.

Together, the words and pictures enables one to form an impression of what seems to be happening or what one would expect to happen. For example, knowing that manager and subordinate (Peter and Margaret) have worked together in a relationship that is smooth, relaxed, comfortable and reciprocal, most people associate the comfortable atmosphere portrayed in Figure 5.1 with Peter and Margaret. Consider the settings themselves for a moment. In Figure 5.1 the two people are not hindered by the imposing bulk of a desk they are literally more open to each other. Contrast this setting with that of Figure 5.2. The desk, massive in relationship to the two participants, suggests a strong barrier that they both need to maintain. Indeed, the narrative indicates that Shelley (the general sales manager) is somewhat uncomfortable in her role, and it is clear that Margaret has erected her own barriers as well. Small wonder that when these two meet, the psychological barriers create physical ones.

This is not to suggest that all managers should immediately burn their desks, light a cigarette, lean back, and *relate*. Consider the situation between Patrick and Mike in figure 5.3. As the story indicates they have less in common than Peter and Margaret. Yet they have a sense of mutual regard related to work issues and, while they still need to seat themselves at a desk, it need not provide an awesome barrier between them as it does for Shelley and Margaret. Beyond the presence or absence of a desk and positioning of persons in relationship to one another, there are a variety of other "staging" issues which the supervisor should consider in planning for the PAI. Foremost of these issues is privacy during the interview. To the extent that the manager and the employee earnestly seek an honest and open exchange during the PAI, the manager must demonstrate his/her concern for privacy. While partitions reaching part way to the ceiling may serve the needs of an economy-minded organization, such physical settings inhibit or even prevent the process of confidential exchange. In such cases, it is wise to secure access to a more private space, such as an unused office or conference room. Clearly, this requires planning on the part of the manager. Such planning is but one of the ways in which the manager shows concern for the interview and ultimately, the employee.

Similarly, while an "open door" policy has much to recommend it—employees value the permission to enter the manager's office as the need arises—during the PAI, the open door should be closed. Phone calls as well defeat interview communication. The manager who allows telephone calls to interrupt the PAI may be reassuring himself that he is important, even indispensable; but he is telling that employee, in effect, that the employee is *not* important. And such interruptions thoroughly prevent on-going dialogue.

Another "staging" issue is the formality or informality of the interview. It is generally a good idea to make the meeting somewhat informal, for several reasons. First, the object of the PAI is to communicate task-relevant information to the employee, and communication proceeds most smoothly when both parties feel comfortable in their surroundings. Secondly, the environment sets the tone for what follows. Research (and our own experience, if we think about it) shows that people form quick reactions to a situation based on the physical setting. If the employee perceived the setting as formal and therefore distant, or even intimidating, the interview will get off to a poor start. Ground lost at the beginning of an interview may never be recovered; and the energy spent getting the interview back on track could have been spent gaining *new* ground.

A relatively informal setting is probably most conducive to communication. However, the supervisor should not do anything highly inconsistent with his normal style. It is vital that *both* parties feel comfortable with the interview environment, for a supervisor who feels ill at ease is certainly not going to put the employee at ease. If the supervisor's normal style is somewhat formal or official, then a highly informal setting may make both people tense and uncomfortable, rather than relaxed. The setting should facilitate communication, not distract from it. A guideline for the interview setting, then, is: be consistent with your normal style, but within the parameters of that style do what you can to make the situation and the setting conducive to quality communication.

Decisions about particular aspects of the setting should be made in light of this guideline. Should the manager encourage the employee to have a cup of coffee or tea during the PAI? This will depend upon the history of the relationship, the personal style of the manager, and the degree of informality the manager wishes to introduce into the interview. Should the employee be encouraged to smoke during the PAI? This will depend upon their relationship and the degree of informality, as well as upon physical factors like the size of the room and the anticipated length of the meeting. If the meeting space is small, the ventilation poor, or the meeting a long one, then smoking may only add to the tension, thus inhibiting communication.

Here, in summary form are the issues relating to PAI settings which the manager should consider:

1. Has proper concern for the privacy of the communications been demonstrated?
    A. Has a meeting place been secured where the verbal exchanges between employee and supervisor cannot be overheard?
    B. Has the privacy of the meeting been secured by closing the door and taking reasonable precautions to assure that there will be no interruptions?
    C. Have arrangements been made regarding telephone messages for both the supervisor and the employee so that neither will be disturbed?
2. Do the seating arrangements (including desk, if any) set the right "tone" and convey the nonverbal message the manager wishes to communicate?
    A. Does the presence of a desk meet the needs of the meeting or of the manager?
    B. Are chairs arranged to encourage or discourage dialogue?
3. Have such "creature comforts" as smoking or coffee been *considered* (even if rejected for practical or historical reasons) by the manager?

NONVERBAL COMMUNICATION: BODY LANGUAGE

The literature on physical communication is as vast as it is varied. Behavioral scientists, for example, have taken motion pictures or videotapes of transactions between persons and analyzed *each frame* of the tapes to study the precise character of the physical communication. Out of such microscopic studies come astonishing bits of cocktail party trivia. For example, did you know that it is possible to discriminate between more than two hundred different types of head nods ranging from those which are barely perceptible to those which are quite vigorous? A moment's reflection reminds us that a barely perceptible head nod (particularly if accompanied by other non-verbal signals such as stroking of chin) may well be interpreted as cautious, provisional acceptance, whereas a vigorous head nod is more apt to be understood as implying strong support and agreement.

Behavioral scientists have invested considerable energy in the attempt to develop a taxonomy of nonverbal behaviors and to promote systematic methods for measuring such behaviors. Meanwhile, the lay public has been treated to a wave of applied nonverbal psychology. Any number of popular paperbacks seem to assure the purchaser that familiarity with the contents will enable him to determine the availability of prospective dating or sexual partners or that careful scrutiny of facial features will provide insights which Freud himself might envy. Still other popularizations claim to provide the reader with subtle and not-so-subtle cues on the ways of using nonverbal language to win-no-matter-what. In this vein, one quasi-religious group has been reported on national television to be training its members in the fine art of staring other persons down. Paired with a trainer the novice begins to stare at the trainer while the trainer starts a stopwatch. Any movement on the part of the novice such as an eye-blink or muscular twitch signals the end of the round and the failure of the novice. The goal of the entire enterprise is reported to be increased capacity for staring at other persons without giving any facial cues. Presumably this leads to greater self-assurance and "power" over other persons. At the least it is apt to make the victim of such a stare uncomfortable.

Any attempt to summarize all the literature on the subject is clearly beyond the scope of this chapter. However, there are a number of aspects of body language that are particularly relevant to the appraisal interview.

What needs to be emphasized about nonverbal, physical communication is: (1) it is a significant vehicle for sending messages; (2) specific physical acts tend to be associated with specific messages; (3) interpretation of physical cues is usually dependent on the context—both verbal and situation—in which the cue is given; (4) it is possible to send one message verbally while sending a totally different message through physical behaviors; and (5) in "mixed message" situations, recipients are more apt to act on the physical message than on the verbal statement. Each of these points will be examined more fully.

1. Body Language Is a Significant Vehicle for Sending Messages

Whether we consider the arms-raised-overhead-clutching-of-hands used by politicians, prize fighters, and other notables to signal victory, the clenched-fist-with-arm-raised to indicate the minority member's desire to fight on, or the irritated passing motorist's extension of a single digit when we cut him off in traffic, nonverbal behavior does communicate. It is an important source of information about our world, at least as important as the verbal messages we receive. The best illustrations of this point lie within the experience of the reader. Set aside some brief part of one day—as little as five minutes will do—to carefully observe the extent to which people use physical means to communicate their messages. Set aside some time too, to become aware of the ways in which you use this "second signal system" to communicate information. As physical messages are woven throughout warp and woof of communication in the everyday world, so do they permeate the interview. The messages we send non-verbally as managers are interpreted no less readily than the words we use.

2. Specific Physical Cues Tend to Be Associated with Specific Messages

Earlier in this chapter three pictures were presented along with narratives describing each situation. Readers were asked to pair the narratives with the pictures. Since verbal cues were not available, nonverbal cues had to be used. A review of these pictures provides an illustration of the statement that specific physical acts tend to be associated with specific messages.

Consider the story about Shelley, the somewhat uncomfortable General Sales Manager, and her resistant, critical salesperson Margaret. The majority of readers will have paired this situation with Figure 5.2. What are the nonverbal cues present in the picture which lead most people to make this linkage? When we ask seminar and workshop participants how they made the association, a number of cues usually emerge.

First, one of the persons, presumably Margaret, is seated in such a manner that her body is not directly facing the other person. In short, she has positioned herself to indicate her wish to avoid contact. Secondly, Margaret has her arms folded across her chest. These nonverbal behaviors are usually interpreted as closed, defensive, or resistant behaviors. Note, too, the line of the mouth on both women—each with a moderate down-turn at the corners: a signal frequently associated with a lack of satisfaction or displeasure. It would come as little surprise to learn (even though we cannot know this from the picture) that one or both clench their jaws tightly when not speaking. In summary, our assessment of this situation can be made on the basis of a number of cues, all of which are highly consistent with one another and lead to the same general interpretation of the situation.

By contrast, consider Figure 5.1. The two central figures are nearly facing one another. Their expressions indicate some degree of pleasure at the encounter. Their hands are not being used to protect and shield; the fingers on the hand of one figure are open rather than clenched. No significant physical barrier exists between the two persons. In short, both appear relatively at ease. Again, the physical cues available in this situation lead most persons to associate the picture with the rewarding relationship of Peter and Margaret.

The frequency with which specific nonverbal behaviors are associated with known data about specific situations indicates there is a commonly shared set of physical acts which carry the same interpretive meaning (at least within a given culture). Thus, if we frown while reading a subordinate's report, it is unlikely that the frown will be interpreted as approval. If we smash our fist on the desk to emphasize a point it is unlikely that we will communicate, "This is not really very important."

More subtly, rearranging papers on the desk while another is talking may be interpreted as lack of attention. Leaning backward to the extent possible or moving your chair farther away from the other party may be interpreted as indifference or even hostility. Conversely, narrowing physical distance (leaning forward, moving the chair slightly forward) is often interpreted as attentiveness, even warmth.

The "non-subtle cue of the year" was related by an editor friend about a visit to a potential client. The client was presented with the editor's business card at the end of their meeting. While escorting the editor to the door, the client proceeded to floss his teeth with the business card, and dropped it in a nearby wastebasket as he bade the editor a warm sincere farewell.

3. Interpretation of Physical Cues is Dependent on the Context

Given that there is a commonly shared nonverbal communication system, that interpretive system is still highly dependent on additional cues. For example, if you overheard the following dialogue with which of the three pictures would you associate the statements?

Person #1 I sure hope the electric company gets that generating plant back on line again. I'm freezing, my office people are freezing, and we're falling further and further behind in the preparation of the Marson Report. I can't ask these employees to work when it's fifty-five degrees in here.

Person #2 You know, this whole thing is depressing to me. Did you know that the generating plant was bombed by some revolutionary group? I heard that on the car radio coming in today. I don't understand what's happening in this country. I just know I don't like it.

In seminars most people match Figure 5.2 with this dialogue. With a different set of supplied facts, what appeared to be hostility, rejection, and disagreement becomes interpreted as despair, disappointment, and frustration. The two figures are not antagonists but, rather, are facing an unpleasant experience which they share in common, although from somewhat different perspectives. One figure has her arms tightly wrapped about her, not because she is striving for distance but because she is engaged in a primordial quest to retain her diminished body heat. In such a situation it is hardly surprising that neither person looks very happy. But their distress is not necessarily directed toward one another.

Still another illustration of the need for supporting cues in order to interpret nonverbal behavior comes from a psychologist friend. During a group therapy session one member revealed an experience that caused him a considerable degree of pain and, in the process, began to weep openly. During the monologue, the psychologist observed another member of the group frequently dabbing at her eyes, clearly in the effort to prevent tears from streaming down her face. After dealing with the first member, he turned to the second person and said, "That story must have touched you deeply. I saw you cry too." The response, to his surprise, was, "No, I've had a minor eye infection for the last few days that makes my eyes water." Thus, what seemed to be an empathetic response to another member's distress was, in fact, a response to a totally different set of stimuli.

4. The Mixed Message: When Physical and Verbal Messages Do Not Match

From time to time we may all need to be reminded that it is possible (but not desirable) to send one message verbally while sending a totally different or highly qualified message through physical behaviors. Thus, the manager who says, "I would like to hear your view on this situation" and then occupies himself with papers on his desk, the view through the window, or the number of acoustical tiles in the ceiling communicates a radically different nonverbal message—to wit, "I am *not* really interested in what you have to say." In this situation, most employees will "hear" the nonverbal message and make their presentation short. They are not apt to forget, however, that they have been made unwilling accomplices in a dishonest exchange which their subordinate position requires they accept, whether the manager acknowledges it or not.

Similarly, the manager who says, "I would like an explanation of this situation" and punctuates the sentence by placing his arms akimbo may be sending a very different message from one who leaves his hands at his side. In the first instance, the message may be interpreted as, "I would like an explanation of this situation *and it had better be good!*" In the second instance, the message may more nearly be, "I would like an explanation of this situation *and I am open to what you have to say.*"

To take another illustration, the manager who responds to an employee's stated desire to take work home over the weekend by answering, "Well, Doris, company policy prohibits employees from taking work home, so I certainly couldn't see you do that," and then giving her a wink and a nob obviates the entire verbal message. The wink says instead, "Doris, I need this work to be done but don't want to be in the position of having given you permission, so I'll look the other way when you leave tonight." If Doris responds only to the verbal message, she may well find herself being ranked down during the PAI for not having the "team spirit" or "caring enough to go the extra mile." Happily, in these conspiratorial mixed communication situations, employees are apt to "get the message," mixed though it may be.

5. When in Doubt Mixed Message Recipients Tend to Act on Physical Cues

As suggested in the first and third example above the nonverbal message is most often the true one; the expression that conveys what the manager really wants and feels, rather than what he thinks he should want or feel. Most persons know this, and given a verbal message that conflicts with the nonverbal message, they will respond to the nonverbal one. The employee whose opinion is verbally solicited and then faces nonverbal message which communicates "I am not really interested in your opinion," will probably offer fewer and briefer opinions across time. And although Doris "got the message," her trust in her employer is apt to suffer.

There is a substantial and growing body of clinical and experimental evidence to support the contention that even relatively minor physical movements (such as head-nods) can alter the verbal behavior of persons. This is particularly true where the message sender is a person of some authority such as a therapist, an experimenter, or a supervisor. In clinical and experimental settings persons have been encouraged to talk more (or less) about themselves, their feelings, their sex life, or other topics of interest, by nothing more than a nod of the head, a change in posture, or a flick of the gaze on the part of the listener. These same dynamic principles of human intercommunication hold no less sway during an encounter as potentially important as the performance evaluation interview.

Here, in summary form, are the issues relating to physical communication in PAI settings which the manager should consider:

1. What nonverbal, physical messages am I sending?

    A. Are these the messages I wish to send?

2. Is my physical communication congruent with my verbal communication (and vice versa)? That is, do both signal systems transmit the same message?

    A. If I am sending mixed messages (one verbal and another, different, physical) what is the *real* message I want to communicate?

3. What nonverbal, physical messages is the employee sending?

    A. What is the impact on the PAI if I am interpreting the nonverbal message correctly?

4. Is the employee's physical communication congruent with his or her verbal communication?

    A. If the employee is sending mixed messages, what is the *real* message?

It would be inappropriate to leave this part of the chapter without addressing some of the questions posed above. What should the manager do if he or she discovers that mixed messages are being communicated? If the supervisor is the one sending the mixed messages, it is difficult to escape the conclusion that the supervisor is not being candid. A supervisory smile, indelibly etched on a steely face, hiding deep and enduring resentments, may enable both parties to survive the direct encounter which a PAI represents. But sometime in the future, if not here and now, both will probably pay a price for maintaining the charade.

The solution to the problem is easy to state but may be difficult to put into practice: *own the behavior and accept responsibility for the message.*

If the employee is sending mixed messages, the supervisor should take the initiative to explore the topic with the employee. The facilitating behaviors discussed earlier in this chapter are useful in ferreting out the meanings behind mixed messages.

V. PLANNING FOR FUTURE PERFORMANCE

Performance appraisal in many organizations tends to focus only upon the past. But we propose that the appraisal process should also be directed at the future, for the following reasons:

"What's done is done." While feedback on past performance is vital, that performance cannot be changed; however, something can be done about performance in the future. Discussion of future performance can motivate employees to perform better by specifying goals for performance and standards for measuring progress.

Finally, discussing future performance orients both manager and employee to the possibilities for improved communication and unit effectiveness.

The extent and nature of performance planning depends upon the level of commitment to performance improvement held by the manager, the subordinate, and the organization. If performance improvement is a matter of indifference, beyond ritual lip service, planning will merely be an exercise.

If improvement of performance is important, planning is greatly facilitated by sound appraisal and thoughtful feedback to the employee by the manager.

The planning element may be a small part of the PAI for most employees, but can be of particular importance for some employees. It is clearly critical for the deficient employee, yet planning is important for the "star" employee as well. Performance objectives (described later), and career objectives stated in terms of training, education, job assignments, etc. can be results of the planning session.

The traditional appraisal process might be depicted as shown below:

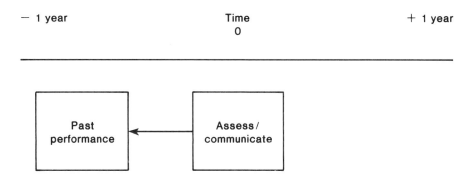

Figure 5.4. Evaluating the past.

Emphasis is placed upon activities from the date of appraisal to one year (usually) in the past.

We suggest instead, the following process:

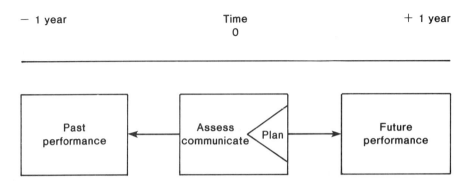

Figure 5.5. Evaluating the past—shaping the future.

Here, emphasis is placed upon "what's next" as well as on the past. Performance goals provide both supervisor and employee with periodic checkpoints for assessing the employee's progress.

PLANNING POSSIBILITIES

Planning possibilities stem from a variety of decisions. Little or no planning is required if both manager and employee are satisfied with the performance level and if previously established objectives are seen as appropriate for the next review period. Figure 5.6 presents such a condition. This situation occurs when the significant characteristics of acceptable job performance have been well defined for some period of time, where the character of the job has changed little and is not expected to change significantly during the next review period, and where the employee (for valid reasons such as proximity to retirement) is not interested in establishing more challenging objectives such as preparation for other jobs or for promotion.

A second possibility for planning is shown in Figure 5.7.

In this case the supervisor perceived a discrepancy between the employee's actual performance and desired performance. The supervisor has communicated these concerns during the performance review period and has provided the employee with an indication of the standards being used to assess his performance. Given these benchmarks, the employee is well aware of the performance discrepancy.

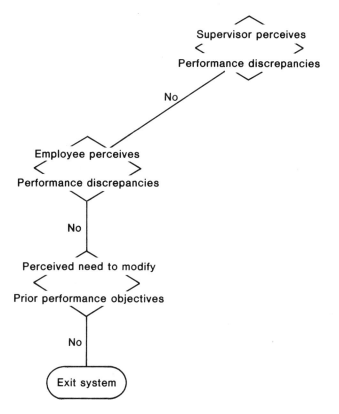

Figure 5.6. Planning possibilities #1.

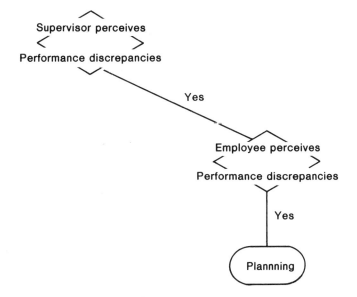

Figure 5.7. Planning possibilities #2.

In these circumstances, when the employee and the supervisor meet, it is clear that one task will be to develop an approach to solving this performance problem. Before real progress can be made, two conditions must be verified:

First, both supervisor and employee must agree that a problem does exist. By providing feedback on a continuing and timely basis throughout the performance review period, the supervisor lays the groundwork for indicating that there is, in fact, a problem.

Secondly, both supervisor and employee must agree that the source of the problem has been defined. Joint planning assumes common efforts toward a commonly defined goal to resolve a commonly defined problem. For example, the supervisor who believes that the match between the job and the employee is the source of the problem is likely to find little agreement from the employee who believes that the problem is in the job itself.

In those situations where there is disagreement between the supervisor and the employee concerning the presence of a problem, the cause of the problem, or the solution to the problem, then negotiation must occur.

In defining the problem, the manager may want to consider the following questions initially:

1. Can the job itself be altered in some way to improve performance? There are many times when the real performance problem is caused by a poorly designed work-flow. There are also performance problems caused by environmental factors such as poor lighting, cramped work areas, etc.

2. Does the job situation provide feedback to the employee? Does the employee know how well or how poorly he/she is doing without having to be told?

3. Is some aspect of the job distasteful? Is the job dirty or unrewarding? Is the job performed at a time of day which disrupts the employee's personal life? Is the work environment physically uncomfortable?

4. Is the employee the problem? Does the employee have the skills to perform the job? This kind of problem is more likely to occur where some aspect of the job has changed during the review period so that new or unpracticed skills are required to perform the job.

5. Will training or retraining improve performance? If the performance problem does involve new or unpracticed skills, can training help? Would retraining help? For example, a supervisor may have received some training in conducting performance evaluation reviews during a supervisory training program two years ago but could now use a refresher course.

6. Will additional practice improve performance? The employee who types or files only infrequently may indeed be a poor performer when pressed into emergency service. Police officers spend a modest amount of time on the firing range to maintain a certain level of proficiency—not because they frequently fire their weapons but because there is always the possibility they may have to fire their weapon. If this is the cause of the problem, periodic practice may need to be scheduled.

7. Is the match between the job and the employee the problem? Is the situation one where an employee with many valuable qualities has been placed in a situation where these positive qualities are not being fully utilized while weaknesses are being accentuated? For example, the best performer is promoted to a supervisory position with no preparation for the promotion. The result is that the organization has gained a supervisor who may be mediocre and has lost a good performer. This is often called the "Peter Principle."
8. Are external factors the problem? Domestic problems, separation, divorce or death of a close friend are known to have a direct relationship to stress. Stress, in turn, can be directly linked to problems in job performance. Financial difficulties, drug/alcohol abuse, and other factors may explain why performance is suffering.

A third kind of planning situation is described in Figure 5.8.

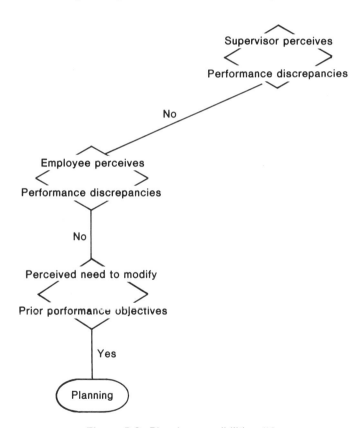

Figure 5.8. Planning possibilities #3.

In this planning situation both the employee and the manager agree that the employee's performance during the prior review period met or exceeded established standards; yet both agree on the need to establish new performance objectives. This situation often occurs with relatively new employees or employees who are "new" to a particular job. Standards appropriate for the trainee may become inappropriate as the employee gains experience and higher standards of performance may have to be devised. Or perhaps a longer-term employee now is seeking additional responsibility as a basis for transfer or promotion. There is no performance discrepancy, but there is a need for additional skills to be mastered to meet the employee's personal goals. This kind of planning is also necessary when the job itself will be changed during the next performance review period. Performance objectives must be changed to accommodate modifications in the job itself.

THE PLANNING PROCESS

Regardless of the situation faced by the manager, the planning process involves the same sequence of activities:

1. Identify the problem or opportunity. A sound appraisal system is a great help here.
2. Develop potential solutions. This may be part of the supervisor's "homework" prior to the feedback session. If training or retraining is required or desired, where will that training be given? Do community colleges, state or local training agencies, etc. offer the required training? Can you, the supervisor, provide the training? These options and others should be considered. Whenever possible the employee should be encouraged to explore solutions.
3. Select "best possible" solution. Criteria to be used for evaluating the potential solutions should be determined jointly by supervisor and employee.
4. Develop implementation plans. This is the essence of the planning portion. Simply stated, this involves a series of questions. Who will do what, and when will it be done? What are the supervisor's responsibilities? What are the employee's responsibilities?
5. Identify performance objectives. Each tentative solution should be stated in terms of a performance objective. The following section describes criteria for writing performance objectives. In essence, the supervisor and employee are developing a performance contract, with each party accepting specific responsibilities.
6. Initiate plan.
7. Evaluate plan. Both parties assure that the other is performing his portion of the solution and periodically review the plan to ascertain if it is, in fact, leading to a solution of the problem.

WRITING PERFORMANCE OBJECTIVES

Creating specific performance objectives is always a good idea. Since job performance occurs over time, and is generally composed of many complex activities, these must be addressed specifically if improvement is desired. The general urging to "do better" is not enough to cause noticeable improvement. Just as one creates a plan for capital investment, a plan for building a home, or a plan for a personal vacation, the supervisor and employee can create a plan for performance improvement. Specific performance objectives are the heart of the administrative system, Management by Objectives; however, even if your organization does not use MBO, defining objectives is of central importance, particularly for employees with performance weaknesses. Such objectives are a logical outcome of the performance appraisal seuqence. Defining them forces employee and supervisor to focus on issues of past performance which have been identified, and guarantees that the PAI helps the employee plan for future progress.

Raters often find it difficult to write performance goals and objectives that convey to the ratee exactly what s/he must do to improve. A good performance objective meets the following criteria: it is specific, pertinent, attainable, measurable, and observable.

Affirmative answers to the following questions will confirm that you have written good performance objective:

Does the objective spell out the who, what, when, where, and how of performance improvement? Are the consequences of performance improvements and lack of improvement spelled out? Is the expected standard of performance in writing? Is it *Specific?*

Is the objective clearly related to job performance? Is it considered important and relevant in the eyes of both supervisor and the subordinate? Does it allow the supervisor and subordinate to focus on the issues of greatest importance? In other words, is it *Pertinent?*

Is it possible to perform at the level being set as the standard? *Attainable?*

How will you know whether or not the employee has acheived this performance goal? What will you measure? Quality? Quantity? Frequency? Efficiency? *Measurable?*

Will you be able to see either the improvement in performance or the result of the improvement in performance? Is it *Observable?*

Readers who have served in the military are familiar with the all-purpose meat product Spam.® To help you remember the requirements of good performance objectives, we offer the mnemonic device "SPAMO"—Specific, Pertinent, Attainable, Measurable, Observable. The more closely the objective meets the SPAMO criteria, the less likely either supervisor or employee is to neglect to clarify what was to be done, when, and by whom.

Both manager and employee should give some thought to the objectives in advance of the PAI. Recognizing that the objectives will be refined after the PAI, it is very useful for both to have a rough draft to discuss. The supervisor should consider having employees frame their own objectives; these can then be reviewed by the supervisor and clarified or adjusted.

It is crucial that performance objectives be stated in writing. While the human memory is an extremely fallible record, written objectives can always be reviewed. Although writing objectives can be a time consuming process, if it is done jointly, it can be a significant step toward improving job performance.

VI INTERVIEW CLOSING

During the final portion of the PAI, the supervisor and employee should attempt to summarize what has been said during the course of the feedback session. This restatement of the important content of the session should cover the following ground:

PERFORMANCE: PAST AND FUTURE

The employee should leave the PAI knowing what objectives (employee behaviors) were seen as most important, what standards were used to evaluate his performance and how well he did in accomplishing the objectives and meeting the standards. The discussion of past performance will probably consume most of the interview, but attention should also be given to the objectives for the next review period and the standards to be used for evaluation. If the standards are the same as for the previous period, state so explicity.

AREAS OF AGREEMENT AND DISAGREEMENT

The employee and supervisor will generally agree on all or most of the topics discussed, especially when good appraisal techniques have been used during the review period.

Agreement should be reached on needed development, what will be done to maintain or improve performance and the resources needed to perform at the desired level.

Areas of disagreement should be acknowledged and discussed.

Once the supervisor has determined—through paraphrasing and feeding back through verbal as well as nonverbal communication—that the above content has been communicated successfully, that concerns on both sides have been expressed, and that the employee understands and agrees to their "contract" for the next period, the appraisal interview is complete.

CHAPTER

6

Concluding Comments

Throughout this book we have stressed the benefits to be gained from a performance appraisal system. We have explored its value as a management technique, its potential for improving overall employee-boss communications, and its worth in promoting productivity. Its value has been proven and is by now generally acknowledged to be an effective technique. Nevertheless, performance appraisal has historically encountered deep-rooted resistance, for a number of well-founded reasons.

Historically, performance appraisal systems have been highly subjective, based on such superficial criteria as personality, appearance, and attitude. The motivation behind the appraisal was often held suspect by managers and employees alike. Many managers viewed appraisals as an unwarranted drain on their most limited resource, namely time. Consequently, performance appraisals were usually sporadic at best—too sporadic to be useful either to the employee or to the organization. It is no surprise that such subjective and infrequent evaluations were viewed skeptically.

Other managers have viewed performance appraisal not merely with skepticism, but with apprehension about possible negative effects. Some have fear that honest appraisal will harm their relationships with their employees. We have often heard the question, "Won't my employees be upset if I tell them they're not doing well?" The answer is a definite "YES!"—if you've been saving this piece of information, storing it away and saying nothing until the review session. A related situation is that of the employee who has been receiving higher-than-deserved evaluations over a number of review periods. This employee has a right to be upset when some rater is finally honest with him or her; but what he should be upset about is not the honesty, but the rater's previous reticence. It is the all-too-frequent lack of ongoing feedback that can make the performance appraisal session an upsetting or destructive experience.

Yet another factor that has bred resistance to the appraisal process is the manner in which it is often implemented within an organization. Some organizations try to put the system into practice much too quickly. It takes time to develop the criteria and standards, train raters in the use of the system, and explain the system to all employees who will be rated. Neglecting any of these stages practically guarantees that employees and managers will resist the system.

Another mistake is ignoring the opinions and needs of employee groups or of their representatives—unions, professional associations, and so on—until too late, after the appraisal system has been "cast in cement." When an appraisal system has been initiated with no regard for their point of view, employees are apt to feel that it has been foisted upon them and to resist it accordingly.

We have seen ample instances where these different forms of resistance surface. Often the resistance is masked in passive forms: unwillingness to subscribe to the philosophy of the appraisal system, refusal to follow the appraisal procedures, avoidance of face-to-face reviews, etc.

The handbill presented in Figure 6.1 is a prime example of the reaction employees might have when they hear, via the grapevine, about a new evaluation system linked to salary actions. One of the authors received this actual handbill from a group of employees who were worried about the impact of merit pay decisions on their own salaries.

This particular group of employees was very concerned that the performance appraisal system would be highly subjective and arbitrary with the resultant salary actions bearing little relation to actual on-the-job performance.

Perhaps the greatest single source of resistance to the performance appraisal process is this lack of understanding regarding the ultimate purpose of appraisal, the obligations of the organization, and the obligations and rights of those being evaluated.

	Quality	Quantity	Attitude	Attendance
John Doe	0	−	+	?
Susan Smith	−	+	?	0
Joseph Brown	+	?	0	−
Mary Jones	?	0	−	+

DON'T LET THIS HAPPEN TO YOU!!!!!!!!!!!!!!

Figure 6.1. An employee view of performance appraisal.

In essence the entire text has addressed methods of overcoming the resistance to appraisal. Central to this theme has been ideas for involving employees in the development of the appraisal system, a thorough orientation of all employees to the appraisal system, and rater training designed to sharpen the appraisal skills of all managers, supervisors, and other raters. The checklist in the following section should serve as a reminder to raters of the critical actions that should be accomplished at each phase of the appraisal process.

AN EVALUATION CHECKLIST

We have mentioned a host of specific actions that should be taken at each stage of the evaluation process. To serve as a summary, we are providing a checklist that divides these actions into five stages:

- Actions to be taken prior to the performance appraisal review period.
- Actions to be taken during the performance appraisal review period.
- Actions to be taken immediately before the feedback session.
- Actions to be taken during the feedback session.
- Actions to be taken immediately after the feedback session.

Raters can use this checklist as a reminder during all phases of the performance appraisal process.

Prior to the performance analysis review period:

_____ Orient employee to the appraisal system

_____ Obtain a job description

_____ Develop objectives, criteria and standards

_____ Assure that employee has a copy of objectives, criteria, and standards.

During the performance analysis review period

_____ Observe employee performance

_____ Keep notes on employee's performance

_____ Provide feedback on a continuing basis through informal evaluation

Immediately before the face-to-face review session

_____ Advise employee that session is pending a few days in advance

_____ Recommend that employee rate self

_____ Review notes related to employee performance

_____ Review prior employee performance on objectives, criteria and standards.

_____ Rate employee on all objectives, criteria, and standards

_____ Plan for specific developmental and/or corrective action

_____ Have second-level reviewer review ratings

During the face-to-face employee feedback/review session

_____ Select a private setting

_____ Involve employee and solicit employee comments

_____ Provide feedback on performance

_____ Prepare an employee development plan

Immediately after the face-to-face review session

_____ Provide employee with a copy of the final signed review

_____ File departmental copy and destroy evaluations after three years

_____ Prepare/modify objectives, criteria, and standards for the next review period

TRAINING OF RATERS

No checklist of actions can guarantee a successful performance appraisal system if those who perform the actions lack the necessary skill. The importance of preparing managers for the all-important task of evaluating performance can not be overemphasized. Any manager who hastily reviews an employee's performance objectives, who makes few, if any, notes on an employee's performance, who is insensitive to the employee's fears and needs during the feedback session, or who treats performance appraisal as a one-way communication tool inadvertently defeats the goals of performance appraisal. Even the most-well-conceived system will eventually be undermined by poorly trained managers.

This book can be an important step in the preparation of managers. Another step of enormous value is formal training. Over the past few years we have had the opportunity to design a number of performance appraisal training programs for managers in a wide variety of organizations. In the process we have learned what constitutes an effective training program. To be of practical value to managers in their day-to-day role as evaluators of their employees a program should:

- Be approximately one day in length. (This could be two half-day sessions or a number of shorter sessions).
- Include a discussion of the rationale behind performance appraisal in general as well as its elements.
- Address the potential evaluators (superior, self, subordinate, peer, etc.) with a recommendation or mandate regarding who must be involved.
- Cover the essential elements of good performance criteria and performance standards
- Present an outline of the performance appraisal feedback session

- Illustrate the preparation and use of an employee development plan
- Analyze rater errors and the reduction or elimination of rater errors
- Give participants an opportunity to role play part of a performance review session.

If videotaping equipment is available, it can be used in conjunction with the role play to offer a very powerful training technique, since videotape is the only economical way to receive complete feedback on exactly what we did and on how we appear to the other person in the review session. Moreover, videotape allows the rater to critique himself or herself after viewing the tape, and this self-critique often adds credibility to the feedback received from others.

With or without training, performance appraisals will occur. Experience and research indicate that effective training impacts both the quality of the appraisals and employee acceptance of the system.

SUMMARY

In this book we have outlined the essential elements of an effective performance appraisal system. We have tried to emphasize the importance of careful preparation and training before implementing the system; and, once implemented, of observing each step in the appraisal process.

Performance appraisal is time-consuming; it may be less than pleasant on occasion; it is true that it requires hard work and commitment to be done properly. There is no question in our minds that the costs in time, training, and learning are significant; but the returns far outweigh the costs. Rather than ask the question of what it costs to do performance appraisals, we suggest that you consider the question of what it costs you to do a poor job of performance appraisal. The wasted resources and lost opportunities as well as the outright expense due to employee dissatisfaction, reduced motivation, wasted ability and potential, higher turnover, and increased recruiting and training activities should more than justify your time and effort to make performance appraisal work!

APPENDIX A

An Employee Manual

Appendix A includes a manual developed by the City of Seattle Personnel Department* to assist in the introduction of their appraisal system to all City employees. It is an excellent example of the kind of material you might want to include in a booklet to orient employees to your system.

Employee's Guide to

Performance Evaluation

Published by

    Training and Performance Systems
    Personnel Department
    City of Seattle
    March, 1979

INTRODUCTION

This Guide will explain the why, what and how of the Performance Evaluation System. As one result of the recently adopted Seattle Personnel Ordinance, the Evaluation System will soon become part of your department's personnel procedures. It is therefore important that you understand the System's purposes and procedures and your role and rights in it.

Your initial reaction to this System will depend, in part, on your past experience with other appraisal systems. Before you read through this booklet, try to identify your concerns and questions about evaluation systems and the evaluation process in general. You will have a chance to learn more about this Performance Evaluation System during your orientation session and later from your supervisor.

*Reprinted with permission.

WHY DO PERFORMANCE EVALUATION?

Formal versus Informal Systems

Even before recorded history, people were being evaluated on their work. Our jobs are a lot different now--more complex and less physically demanding, but some aspects of work do not change. We still have deadlines. We must gain the required knowledge and perfect the necessary skills to do our work. And no matter who we are or what we do, someone is assessing how well we are doing our job.

We spend a lot of time sizing up situations, other people--and ourselves. You make daily appraisals about the food you eat, the music you hear, the books you read, the television programs you watch, the clothes people wear and much more. Appraising people and things around you is almost as natural as breathing. You do it at home--and at work.

During each work day you spend a lot of time sizing up your own work, deciding whether you are satisfied with it. You also observe the work done by your co-workers, your supervisor, and perhaps people outside your work area. At the same time, your co-workers, supervisor and perhaps others are watching and assessing you. This is a constant appraisal process, which happens in an informal way.

The problem with these casual assessments is that they are generally not discussed, or even written down. In addition, they may not be based on work related criteria. Yet decisions about your present and future job status sometimes use these elusive, unspoken evaluations.

A formal, written appraisal system brings your supervisor's assessments of your work into the open where you can comment, clarify and give input. The Performance Evaluation System is a structured process which provides both written and verbal evaluations of your work. Unlike informal evaluations, the Performance Evaluation System is based on job related criteria, and offers a way to make evaluations open and fair.

Purposes of this System

The most commonly asked questions about a performance appraisal system are: Why are we doing it? What is it supposed to accomplish? The Performance Evaluation System was designed to be an ongoing process that will accomplish three things:

--serve as an assessment tool for job performance,
--provide better communication between supervisors and employees, and
--serve as a useful guide for personnel actions.

As an assessment tool the evaluation results will show both supervisors and employees their strong and weak areas. You will know how your job performance compares with job related criteria. Communication will be enhanced because you will have a chance to discuss your work and find ways to improve it.

Finally, the City's Personnel Ordinance allows the use of evaluation results to "help demonstrate cause for personnel actions." In most cases this will happen only after the System has been in place for one year.

WHAT IS PERFORMANCE EVALUATION?

An Overview of the System

Before reading about the Performance Evaluation System in more detail, look at the chart below and read the definitions of some of the terms you will hear.

Performance Evaluation Cycle

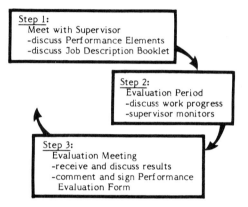

At the beginning of each cycle, you will review the Performance Elements and Job Description Booklet, and update the Booklet if necessary.

Definitions

Performance Element: A knowledge or skill required to do a job.

Job Description Booklet: A booklet containing the Performance Elements for your evaluation group. You and your supervisor write examples of how you use each Element in your job. These examples are called work activity examples.

Work Activity Example: A task or duty you perform as part of your job.

Evaluation Period: The time between the first meeting with your supervisor and the evaluation meeting; usually six months.

Performance Evaluation Form: The form on which your evaluation is recorded. It has a list of Performance Elements with room for signatures and comments at the end. You are rated on each Element at the end of the evaluation period.

Evaluation Group: A group of employees who use the same Performance Elements because their jobs require the same knowledge and skills. There is a different list of Performance Elements for each of the 33 evaluation groups.

Rater: The person who evaluates your work performance; almost always your supervisor.

Reviewer: The person who will review your Performance Evaluation Form after you and your supervisor have discussed it. This person is usually your supervisor's supervisor.

An Explanation of the System

Performance Evaluation is a job related appraisal system which was developed by City employees. It provides a different set of evaluation criteria, called Performance Elements, for each major type of work in the City. Prior to starting the evaluation cycle, you and your supervisor complete a Job Description Booklet. This entails listing sample work activities for each Element.

You will receive this Booklet during an orientation session. This is also the time when you hear an explanation of the System and can ask questions. Following this orientation session, you and your supervisor will start the evaluation process, which has three steps.

First, the two of you will meet to discuss the Performance Elements and your Job Description Booklet. Following this meeting, the second step begins - the evaluation period itself. This is usually six months long, but may be shorter for probationary employees. During this time you and your supervisor will discuss how things are going. Your supervisor will be monitoring and observing your performance so he/she can make a fair and accurate evaluation.

The third step in the evaluation process occurs at the end of the evaluation period. You again meet with your supervisor and receive your evaluation results. You will be evaluated on the Performance Elements, not the Job Description Booklet. You and your supervisor will discuss ways to use the information for improving your work, utilizing your strengths, and possibly changing work assignments.

After this discussion, you and your supervisor sign the evaluation form. Your signature means that you have seen and discussed your evaluation results, not that you agree with them. You may write your reaction to your evaluation in the comment section. A comment is strongly encouraged if you do not totally agree with the evaluation results. A reviewer (a person other than your supervisor who is familiar with your work) will read over the form. This person will look into instances when the employee is not satisfied with the evaluation.

After the evaluation meeting, it is time to start the next evaluation cycle. You will have a chance to review and update the Job Description Booklet and will talk again with your supervisor about the Performance Elements.

The next two sections in this Guide will give you more information about the actual parts of the Performance Evaluation System.

Performance Elements

Performance Elements describe the knowledge and skills required to do one's job. Knowledge and skills are the physical and mental actions a person goes through in performing a task (work activity), or part of one's job. For example, the task of setting up a filing system requires at least two skills: skill in planning and organizing work and skill in understanding and applying procedures and instructions.

It is important to realize that the task (work activity) is not the same as the knowledge or skill required to carry it out. You use or apply knowledge and skills to do the various tasks (activities) in your job. Performance Elements describe the knowledge and skills -- not the tasks or work activities. You will be evaluated on how well you demonstrate the knowledge and skills.

Some examples of Performance Elements are:

--skill in meeting deadlines
--skill in cooperating with others
--skill in scheduling and assigning work
--knowledge of relevant codes, ordinances and guidelines
--knowledge of departmental policies

Because different jobs require different knowledge and skills, we developed Performance Elements for each of the 33 major types of work in the City. These major types of work, or Performance Evaluation Groups, consist of similar job classes. You will find out which group you are in during your orientation session and later you will have an opportunity to study the Elements for your job.

You may be interested to know that the method used to develop the Elements is unique because the employees who actually do the work provided the information. A representative profile of employees from each evaluation group participated in Job Element analysis sessions (this profile included employees from all levels in the group, not just supervisors.)

The sessions were, in effect, small group discussions. The participants identified the knowledge and skills required to do their type of work. Then, through a rating process that identified those items the group thought most necessary to good performance, they developed a list of Performance Elements. A structured editing process followed to insure that the Elements were observable and well stated.

You will have an opportunity to discuss the Elements for your job during the first meeting with your supervisor. A particular Element may not be required in your specific job; in that case, you and your supervisor may agree to eliminate it from the list.

Job Description Booklet

You recall that Performance Elements describe the knowledge and skills you use to do your job. The Job Description Booklet you receive will list the Performance Elements for your evaluation group. Under each Element in the Booklet, you will write a few brief statements describing the work activities (tasks) in which you use that knowledge or skill.

In other words, the Job Description Booklet is a list of Performance Elements for your evaluation group, and the work activities that show how these Performance Elements apply to your particular job. An example of a Performance Element and some of the work activities in which it is used is shown below:

Demonstrates skill in meeting deadlines in the following ways:

<u>Process</u>   <u>vouchers</u>
(action verb)   (what)

<u>in order to meet payroll deadlines</u>
(why or what's accomplished)

<u>Write</u>   <u>progress memos</u>
(action verb)   (what)

<u>in order to keep supervisor informed</u>
(why or what's accomplished)

<u>Complete</u>   <u>Federal reporting forms</u>
(action verb)   (what)

<u>in order to meet Federal deadlines/
keep Federal money</u>
(why or what's accomplished)

You will receive your Job Description Booklet during your orientation session. The instructor will show you how to fill it out and you will be given time to complete it on your own. This is one of your opportunities to give input to the evaluation process.

This Booklet will then be reviewed by your supervisor to make this a joint effort between the two of you. Because your supervisor is responsible for defining and guiding your work, he/she has the final responsibility for your Booklet and may modify what you have written or add examples of other work activities.

The Job Description Booklet will be a reflection of your job as it develops and changes. Modifications on it will be ongoing. At the beginning of each evaluation period you and your supervisor will review, discuss and update the Booklet. Even with additions, it will contain only the most important work activities. It will probably never contain <u>all</u> your tasks.

The Job Description Booklet serves several purposes. It clarifies how you use the knowledge and skills described in the Performance Elements. It serves as a document to satisfy Federal Government requirements. And, if you leave your job, it will go to the person filling your position, giving him/her a good idea of what your job is all about.

WHAT ARE YOUR ROLE AND RIGHTS?

The Performance Evaluation System is designed as a two-way process between you and your supervisor. Your supervisor's role will be to communicate with you about your job and to evaluate your performance. You have a defined role in this system too.

Your Role

First, you will be asked to give careful, accurate input when completing your Job Description Booklet. Second, you will discuss your job performance with your supervisor during the evaluation period. Your responsibility is to ask for clarification when something about your job is not clear and to point out problems when they occur. If you find you would like more feedback from your supervisor about how you are doing -- ask.

The third part of your role is to express your views about your job and the evaluation results. To state your honest views may sometimes be difficult, but it is important. The <u>two</u>-way evaluation process works only if you say what you think.

Your Rights

You also have definite rights in this System. First, you have the right to know what is expected of you, that is, the right to see and discuss the Performance Elements on which you will be evaluated. This includes the right to discuss how your work is going during the evaluation period.

You have the right to know your supervisor's assessments of your work. Throughout the evaluation period, your supervisor should be giving you feedback on your work. At the end of the period, you will receive a written evaluation.

Finally, you have the right to appeal ratings you receive. At the orientation session, you will be informed of the appeal procedure developed by your department.

The Performance Evaluation System is a dynamic, ongoing process and you are an integral part of it. If you fulfill your role and exercise your rights you will help insure that this Performance Evaluation System works to benefit you, as well as your department and the City.

APPENDIX B

An Essay Appraisal Form

Appendix B includes an example of a very detailed essay-type performance appraisal. This appraisal addresses performance in relation to objectives (which are specified elsewhere), significant accomplishments, skills being used on the job, skills not being used on the job, performance ratings, employee development plan, support of the company affirmative action program, and promotability. This system also includes self-evaluation since the first section is completed by the employee being evaluated.

EXEMPT
PERFORMANCE REVIEW
AND
DEVELOPMENT PLAN

NAME _____

POSITION _____

DIVISION/DEPARTMENT _____

LOCATION _____

TIME IN CURRENT ASSIGNMENT _____

REVIEW PERIOD – FROM: _____ TO: _____

Instructions: This review is designed to be completed in two steps.

1. The EMPLOYEE completes SECTION I.
2. The SUPERVISOR completes SECTIONS II - V, obtains the required signatures, discusses the review with the employee and forwards the completed review to Personnel.

Supervisor _____

Review Date _____

(Use additional sheets as required.)

SECTION I

TO THE EMPLOYEE

READ THE PERFORMANCE REVIEW AND DEVELOPMENT PLAN HANDBOOK BEFORE YOU ATTEMPT TO COMPLETE THIS SECTION.

A. Utilizing your objectives for this review period, list the most important performance functions of your job.

B. Now, list your accomplishments within the above performance functions during this review period.

C. Referring to your objectives and accomplishments, list the skills, education, and training you are using in your job:

_____
_____
_____
_____
_____
_____
_____
_____
_____
_____
_____
_____
_____
_____
_____
_____

D. Now list and describe the skills and knowledge that you possess that you could use here at   if given the opportunity. Include here also those things that you would like to do at

_____
_____
_____
_____
_____
_____
_____
_____
_____
_____
_____
_____
_____
_____
_____
_____

Employee Signature _____

Date _____

SECTION II

THE EVALUATION

TO THE SUPERVISOR: DO NOT ATTEMPT TO COMPLETE THIS REVIEW UNTIL YOU HAVE READ AND UNDERSTAND THE PERFORMANCE REVIEW AND DEVELOPMENT PLAN HANDBOOK.

THIS PERFORMANCE REVIEW REQUIRES THAT YOU RATE YOUR SUBORDINATE ACCORDING TO SPECIFIC STANDARDS AND OBJECTIVES ESTABLISHED FOR THE POSITION. THESE OBJECTIVES SHOULD BE CLEARLY OUTLINED, QUANTIFIED WHEREVER POSSIBLE, WITH TARGET DATES ESTABLISHED FOR THEIR COMPLETION. A LIST OF THESE OBJECTIVES SHOULD BE ATTACHED TO THIS REVIEW.

A. List and comment on areas where accomplishments have met or exceed expectations.

_____

B. List areas where accomplishments have been less than anticipated.

_____

SECTION III

IMPROVEMENT PLAN

Make comments on those areas of performance that need improvement and identify a development plan.

A. Using your list in Section IIB, comment on how the employee can improve his/her performance to meet established goals.

    _____
    _____
    _____
    _____
    _____
    _____
    _____
    _____
    _____
    _____
    _____
    _____
    _____
    _____
    _____

B. Outline below a program for addtional growth within the company. Considerations may include courses to take, conferences to attend, special assignments, cross training, seminars, community activities, professional organizations, etc.

    _____
    _____
    _____
    _____
    _____
    _____
    _____
    _____
    _____
    _____
    _____
    _____
    _____
    _____
    _____

SECTION IV

PERFORMANCE RATING AND COMMENTS

A. Based upon the described position responsibilities and performance factors, evaluate the employee in terms of overall impact and effectiveness in the job by placing an X at the appropriate place on the performance bar.

PERFORMANCE BAR

Unsatisfactory	Average			Outstanding
	Below	Median	Above	

B. Make additional comments to explain the overall rating. Also comment on unusual circumstances that may have affected the performance, and on other factors pertinent to the employee and the position.

_____
_____
_____
_____
_____
_____
_____
_____
_____
_____
_____
_____

C. If this employee supervises others; please comment on the employee's contributions and future plans for supporting Affirmative Action Program.

_____
_____
_____
_____
_____
_____
_____
_____
_____
_____
_____
_____

SECTION V

PROMOTABILITY AND SUMMARY

A. Promotability - based upon the appraisal of the employee's performance and other related factors evaluate the employee in terms of promotability.

      _____ Barely adequate or less at present level of responsibility.

      _____ Has reached maximum growth at present level of responsibility.

      _____ Capable of assuming lateral responsibility.

      _____ Capable of assuming higher level of responsibility.

      _____ Other

Comments on short term potential

Comments on long term potential

B. APPROVALS:

Supervisor's Signature _____ Date: _____

Reviewed by _____ Date: _____

Dept. Head Review _____ Date: _____

Personnel Dept. Review _____ Date: _____

C. Employee Comments:

_____
_____
_____
_____
_____
_____
_____
_____
_____
_____
_____
_____
_____
_____

Employee Signature _____ Date: _____

(Signature of employee does not signify agreement with the review, but indicates that the review process has been completed.)

EMPLOYEE: _____

THE PERFORMANCE TRACKING RECORD

To the Supervisor:

Record events or factors that will help you complete the next annual performance review and development plan. Separate this form from the review and maintain all tracking records in one loose leaf binder for easy reference. Note that these entries should be made at the time they occur.

Supervisor _____

Next Review Date: _____

Item: Date:

APPENDIX C

Management by Objectives and Criteria-only Form

Appendix C presents an example of a combination of two approaches to performance appraisal. The first section of this appraisal form represents a management by objectives system that requires performance standards to be developed for each of the objectives. The second part of the form is a criteria-only approach which is designed to be personalized for each person being rated by requiring the rater to specify criteria in Parts B and C.

Reprinted with permission.

SALARIED EMPLOYEE PERFORMANCE REVIEW

POSITION OBJECTIVES FOR PERIOD _____, 19_____ through _____, 19_____

OBJECTIVES OF _____
                     (Employee)

POSITION TITLE _____

DEPARTMENT _____

DIVISION _____

SUPERIOR _____

POSITION PURPOSE _____

_____

_____

_____

_____

_____

_____

_____

CRITICAL WORK AREAS AND SPECIFIC OBJECTIVES	STANDARDS	TARGET DATES	
		Planned	Actual
From your Position Charter or Position Description, list, in order of importance, the Critical Work Areas of your position. These are the major areas of work for which you are accountable on an on-going basis. For each area of Critical Work, state specifically the results you plan to accomplish during the 12-month period. **For Example:** **CLAIMS PROCESSING.** 1. To process professional claims in accord with the established procedures and time limits.	For each specific result that you have listed, indicate the measure, either as a quantity or a quality, that will indicate the manner in which the end result will be achieved in a **proficient** manner. **For Example:** **CLAIMS PROCESSING.** An annual average of 250 claims per day per employee will be processed at an average cost of $2.28 per claim.		

PERFORMANCE REVIEW				
PERIOD ENDING: _____ based on completion of objectives to date				
ACHIEVEMENT LEVEL				COMMENTS FOR REVIEW
Exceeded	Achieved	Partially Met	Little Or No Action	Use this column to support the achievement level indicated. If revisions are made on the original objectives and standards, state the reason and adjustment here.

CRITICAL WORK AREAS AND SPECIFIC OBJECTIVES	STANDARDS	TARGET DATES	
		Planned	Actual
From your Position Charter or Position Description, list, in order of importance, the Critical Work Areas of your position. These are the major areas of work for which you are accountable on an on-going basis. For each area of Critical Work, state specifically the results you plan to accomplish during the 12-month period. **For Example:** **CLAIMS PROCESSING.** 1. To process professional claims in accord with the established procedures and time limits.	For each specific result that you have listed, indicate the measure, either as a quantity or a quality, that will indicate the manner in which the end result will be achieved in a **proficient** manner. **For Example:** **CLAIMS PROCESSING.** An annual average of 250 claims per day per employee will be processed at an average cost of $2.28 per claim.		

SIGNATURES

Employee _____ Date _____

Superior _____ Date _____

Reviewed by _____ Date _____

PERFORMANCE REVIEW

PERIOD ENDING: _____
based on completion of objectives to date

ACHIEVEMENT LEVEL				COMMENTS FOR REVIEW
Exceeded	Achieved	Partially Met	Little Or No Action	Use this column to support the achievement level indicated. If revisions are made on the original objectives and standards, state the reason and adjustment here.

UNPLANNED ACCOMPLISHMENTS: List other accomplishments achieved by employee not listed above.

WORK RELATED SKILLS AND KNOWLEDGE

This section evaluates the skills, knowledge, and techniques an employee applies in achieving the desired job objective. Using the standards indicated below, rate the employee's performance in the evaluation.

CODE	RATING	STANDARDS FOR REVIEW
1.	Distinguished:	Performance and achievements far exceed the position's requirements in all respects.
2.	Commendable:	Performance is noticeably better than required by the position. Achievements have been accomplished occasionally above normal requirements for the position.
3.	Proficient:	Performance meets the position's requirements. Achievements are at a level normally expected for the position.
4.	Provisional:	Performance sometimes meets the position's requirements. Achievements are often below that normally expected for an individual in the position.
5.	Marginal:	Performance often falls short of the position's requirements in one or more significant areas. Achievements are constantly below that expected for the postion.

A. Management Skills

PERIOD ENDING _____

1. **Planning** - the work a manager performs to predetermine a course of action.   1 2 3 4 5

2. **Organizing** - the work a manager performs to arrange and relate the work to be done so it can be performed effectively by people.   1 2 3 4 5

3. **Leading** - the work a manager performs to influence people to take effective action.   1 2 3 4 5

4. **Controlling** - the work a manager performs to assess and regulate work in progress and to assess the results secured.   1 2 3 4 5

WORK RELATED SKILLS AND KNOWLEDGE	
B. Technical Skills and Knowledge Describe below the specific technical skills and knowledge required to perform this position. Evaluate the degree of proficiency the employee demonstrates in applying these to the job objectives. **Skill:** **Skill:** **Skill:** **Skill:** **Comments:**	PERIOD ENDING_____ 1 2 3 4 5 1 2 3 4 5 1 2 3 4 5 1 2 3 4 5

C. Additional Performance Criteria

List here and comment on any other factors you believe to be relevant in evaluating this employee's performance.

PROFESSIONAL DEVELOPMENT PLAN

In developing this plan, consider on-the-job experiences, courses, professional associations and activities that will assist the employee in increasing skills and knowledge required for the current position and to prepare to achieve future career goals.

DEVELOPMENT OBJECTIVES	DATE COMPLETED	COMMENTS

OVERALL PERFORMANCE EVALUATION: PERIOD ENDING _____

This section summarizes the employee's overall performance during the reviewed period. It is based on your evaluation of the completed job objectives, the application of work related skills and knowledge, and the additional performance criteria. Indicate the appropriate level below.

| 1 DISTINGUISHED | 2 COMMENDABLE | 3 PROFICIENT | 4 PROVISIONAL | 5 MARGINAL |

Comments:

SIGNATURES

Employee _____ Date _____

Superior _____ Date _____

Reviewed by _____ Date _____

EMPLOYEE COMMENTS   **PERIOD ENDING:** _____

Employee Signature   Date

APPENDIX

D

Form Adaptable to Most Approaches

The evaluation system displayed in Appendix D can be any type of system that the rater chooses. In the section on performance criteria, the rater can use a management by objectives approach, a criteria-only approach, or a criteria and standards approach. Section C of Part I presents eighteen criteria that are common to many managerial jobs. The rater has the option of using some, all, or none of these criteria. Section D of Part I is an interesting method of documenting the quarterly interim reviews that occur throughout the year. Part II, Section A is the self-evaluation component of this appraisal system. Section B of Part II is the supervisor appraisal format.

Reprinted with permission.

RainierBancorporation
PERFORMANCE APPRAISAL FORMS

Supervisors:

Through Performance Appraisal, you and your employee will determine and document expected job performance and achieved results. Program instructions are in the Reference Guide, People Section. Further assistance is available from your manager, your area operations/personnel specialists, or from the Compensation Department.

OVERVIEW:

PERFORMANCE APPRAISAL ASKS:	THE CORRESPONDING STEPS/FORMS ARE:	PAGE NO.
1. What Needs to be Done? (defining expected performance.)	I. PERFORMANCE CRITERIA FORM:	
	A. JOB STANDARDS: describing regular, recurring tasks and responsibilities.	I-A-1
	B. SPECIFIC OBJECTIVES: for nonrecurring, one-time projects, goals, targets.	I-B-1
	C. COMMON FACTORS: to supplement standards and objectives or serve as a basis for general discussions of important skills or attributes.	I-C-1
2. Is it Getting Done? (monitoring performance.)	D. INTERIM REVIEWS: to record performance-to-date between formal appraisals.	I-D-1

Note: The Criteria Form (I) may be used as designed or you may devise your own system which achieves the same intent and results.

3. Did it Get Done? (assessing results.)	II. PERFORMANCE APPRAISAL FORM: (worksheets & final copy.)	
	A. EMPLOYEE ASSESSMENT: of results achieved compared to established criteria.	II-A-1 & II-A-2
	B. SUPERVISOR ASSESSMENT: including related questions and overall rating.	II-B-1 THRU II-B-3
	C. DEVELOPMENTAL PLAN (as needed), EMPLOYEE COMMENTS (optional), SIGNATURES (required).	II-C-1

Note: The Appraisal Form (II parts A & B) become the approved document that is to be kept in the employee's file. The questions are designed to cover most situations. Reasonable interpretation or modification of a section(s) is permitted to meet the needs of the specific job, location, supervisor, or employee.

RAINIER BANCORPORATION

I. PERFORMANCE CRITERIA
A. JOB STANDARDS

FOR (EMPLOYEE)		DATE
JOB TITLE	SUPERVISOR	

Here are the job standards we will use to evaluate your performance of regular, recurring tasks and responsibilities at your next performance appraisal in _____ (Month, Year).
(Indicate/discuss relative importance of each item.)

STANDARDS

(Add pages as needed. Note and review changes or revisions as they occur.)

EMPLOYEE INITIAL	SUPERVISOR INITIAL

RAINIER BANCORPORATION

I. PERFORMANCE CRITERIA
B. SPECIFIC OBJECTIVES

Here are the specific objectives we will use to measure your performance on nonrecurring projects and target goals at your next performance appraisal in _____ *(Month, Year)*. *(Indicate/discuss relative importance of each.)*

SPECIFIC OBJECTIVES

(Add pages as needed. Note and review changes or revisions as they occur.)

EMPLOYEE INITIAL	SUPERVISOR INITIAL

RAINIER BANCORPORATION

I. PERFORMANCE CRITERIA
C. COMMON PERFORMANCE FACTORS

We will consider the common performance factors checked here in monitoring and evaluating your job performance. These will be considered in addition to, not a replacement for, job standards and objectives.

(Note: Selection of factors is optional unless critical to job performance or managerial responsibilities. Factors may be used to highlight generally useful skills or attributes.)

COMMON PERFORMANCE FACTORS	COMMENTS
☐ **QUALITY** - of finished work regardless of amount completed. Accuracy, neatness, thoroughness.	
☐ **QUANTITY** - amount of satisfactory work completed. Volume of output, speed in completing assignments.	
☐ **TIME MANAGEMENT** - meeting deadlines. Utilizing time effectively for maximum output and/or highest quality. Punctuality. Attendance.	
☐ **ORGANIZATION** - logically plans and organizes own and/or others' work for most effective handling or reduction of unnecessary activities.	
☐ **COMMUNICATIONS** - Effectiveness of written, oral, listening skills.	
☐ **KNOWLEDGE OF OWN JOB** - know-how and skills necessary to do the job. Adequacy of practical, technical, or professional skills and experience.	
☐ **KNOWLEDGE OF RELATED AREAS** - awareness of work relationships with other areas.	
☐ **LEADERSHIP** - ability, skills in orienting, motivating, guiding others. Serving as a good example. Optimum use of staff other resources to complete task, achieve a goal.	
☐ **SELF-DEVELOPMENT** - awareness of own strengths, weaknesses, interests. Plans for elimination of deficiencies, attainment of goals. Accepts/seeks new responsibilities.	
☐ **SELF-STARTER** - working with limited supervision or direction. Following through on own initiative.	
☐ **HUMAN RELATIONS** - effective work relations with supervisor, peers, others outside working unit, favorable customer relations.	
☐ **PLANNING** - setting objectives, budgeting, scheduling, forecasting.	
☐ **DECISION MAKING** - making prompt decisions considering relevant factors and evaluating alternatives.	
☐ **COST AWARENESS** - awareness of financial impact of decisions, actions. Good business judgment.	
☐ **DEVELOPING PEOPLE** - Recognizing growth potential, development of opportunities, skill in coaching and counseling. Fair and consistent use of discipline. Respect for the individual.	
☐ **PERSONNEL PRACTICES** - effective and appropriate use of salary and benefits programs, performance appraisal, internal placement, career planning, training and development opportunities, etc.	
☐ **AFFIRMATIVE ACTION** - working with others harmoniously without regard to race, religion, national origin, sex, age, or handicap. Seeking ways to achieve organizational EEO objectives and timetables. Actively seeking to enhance career objectives of minorities, women and handicapped people.	
☐ **SUPPORT OF SOCIAL POLICY, CONSUMER AFFAIRS PROGRAMS** - professional, community, or volunteer activities which promote company objectives. Actively promoting Affirmative Lending and other consumer programs.	
☐ **OTHER** -	
☐ **OTHER** -	

RAINIER BANCORPORATION

I. PERFORMANCE CRITERIA
D. INTERIM REVIEWS

(Use this page or similar documentation to record performance-to-date between formal appraisals.)

FIRST REVIEW   DATE _____

EMPLOYEE INITIAL   SUPERVISOR INITIAL

SECOND REVIEW   DATE _____

EMPLOYEE INITIAL   SUPERVISOR INITIAL

THIRD REVIEW   DATE _____

EMPLOYEE INITIAL   SUPERVISOR INITIAL

RAINIER BANCORPORATION **II. PERFORMANCE APPRAISAL**
A. EMPLOYEE ASSESSMENT

FOR(EMPLOYEE)	JOB TITLE
LOCATION	SUPERVISOR
TIME IN JOB	PERFORMANCE PERIOD: FROM TO

(Note: Final copy must be accompanied by Part II.B.: Supervisor Assessment)

EMPLOYEE ASSESSMENT

Here is how I see my performance in relation to Standards and Objectives since my last appraisal.

EMPLOYEE ASSESSMENT (Continued)

I have shown greatest strength or improvement in performing my job in these areas:

I would like to improve my performance on the job in these areas:

These are my objectives for this job, or for a career, or for my own improvement, for now and in the future.
OR: ☐ At this time, I am satisfied in my, current position and wish to remain.
(Note: This section is optional. By noting your interest, even if they change later on, your supervisor can provide counseling and direction to help you reach your goals.)

Here are ways that would help me improve my performance or meet my objectives (e.g., more or different help from your supervisor, special training in basic or new skills, cross-training in other areas, etc.).

RAINIER BANCORPORATION

II. PERFORMANCE APPRAISAL
B. SUPERVISOR ASSESSMENT

FOR (EMPLOYEE)	PERFORMANCE PERIOD
	FROM: TO:

(Note: Final copy must be accompanied by Part II.A.: Employee Assessment)

SUPERVISOR ASSESSMENT	EXPECTED LEVEL OF PERFORMANCE		
Here is how I see your performance in relation to the Standards and Objectives we agreed to. *(Indicate/discuss relative importance of each.)*	Exceeds	Meets	Does Not Meet

SUPERVISOR ASSESSMENT (Continued)

ACHIEVEMENT OF STANDARDS AND OBJECTIVES - *(Continued)*	EXPECTED LEVEL OF PERFORMANCE		
	Exceeds	Meets	Does Not Meet

COMMON PERFORMANCE FACTORS			
Here's how I see your performance in relation to the Common Performance Factors we set at the beginning of this appraisal cycle. *(Omit if none previously selected.)*	EXPECTED LEVEL OF PERFORMANCE		
	Exceeds	Meets	Does Not Meet

SUPERVISOR ASSESSMENT (Continued)

Here are what I see as your major strengths and abilities, the things you've done particularly well, and the significant improvements you've made since your last appraisal:

I think improvement in these areas will increase your overall effectiveness on the job: *(Explain)*

I also considered these additional factors (if any) in reaching the overall rating for you:

OVERALL PERFORMANCE

Here's how I rate your overall performance, based on the performance criteria we established and considering the relative importance of each:

DOES NOT MEET EXPECTED LEVEL OF PERFORMANCE ☐   MEETS EXPECTED LEVEL OF PERFORMANCE ☐   EXCEEDS EXPECTED LEVEL OF PERFORMANCE ☐

RAINIER BANCORPORATION   **II. PERFORMANCE APPRAISAL**
                                              C. PLAN AND REVIEW

DEVELOPMENTAL PLAN

I think we should take these steps to improve your performance on the job, or to help you progress toward your personal career objectives.

(Use this space or separate documentation as needed or as requested by the employee. Consider career planning, training and development programs, and external courses.)

EMPLOYEE COMMENTS

What do you think about this appraisal? *(Optional.)*

_____   _____
EMPLOYEE SIGNATURE   DATE

(Signature indicates you have seen and discussed this appraisal with your supervisor. It does not necessarily imply agreement with the appraisal or overall rating.)

_____   _____
SUPERVISOR'S SIGNATURE   DATE

_____   _____
REVIEWED BY   DATE

_____   _____
ADDITIONAL REVIEW - *(As required)*   DATE

APPENDIX

Criteria and Standards Form

Appendix E includes examples of criteria and standards developed for the following jobs and job families:
1. Department heads
2. Secretary
3. Budget Coordinator
4. Animal Technician
5. Administrative Assistant
6. Senior Operator in a Sewage Treatment Plant
7. Schedule Maker in a Transit System

EMPLOYEE PERFORMANCE EVALUATION RATING DOCUMENT

for position of

D E P A R T M E N T H E A D

THE PURPOSE OF THIS PERFORMANCE EVALUATION SCALE IS TO PROVIDE AN OBJECTIVE WAY OF EVALUATING THE POSITION OF DEPARTMENT HEAD. THE RATING SCALES WHICH FOLLOW HAVE BEEN DESIGNED TO HELP RATE THE PERFORMANCE IN 15 AREAS WHICH HAVE BEEN CONSISTENTLY IDENTIFIED AS IMPORTANT ASPECTS OF THE DEPARTMENT HEAD'S JOB.

EACH PAGE CONTAINS A PERFORMANCE CRITERION, ITS DEFINITION, AND A RATING SCALE MADE UP OF A SERIES OF STATEMENTS WHICH HAVE BEEN NUMBERED FROM "0" THROUGH "5". THE PURPOSE OF THE BEHAVIOR STATEMENTS IS TO GIVE EXAMPLES OF THE LEVEL OF PERFORMANCE INDICATED BY THE VARIOUS SCALE NUMBERS.

CONSIDER THE INDIVIDUAL TO BE RATED AND GIVE A RATING ON EACH OF THE 15 CRITERIA OF PERFORMANCE. KEEPING IN MIND THE DEFINITION OF THE CRITERIA, RATE THE INDIVIDUAL BY HOW WELL HE/SHE TYPICALLY PERFORMS EACH JOB ASPECT.

CRITERION 1: COMMUNICATION SKILLS

This criterion measures the degree to which department heads communicate ideas, suggestions, programs, projects, etc., both orally & in writing, to diverse audiences (e.g., peers, superiors, subordinates, public, etc.)

THESE STATEMENTS DESCRIBE PERSONS WHO ARE USUALLY RATED OUTSTANDING ON COMMUNICATION SKILLS

(5) --Always communicates (written & oral) ideas, presentations, projects, etc., in a clear, objective, organized manner to all audiences

--Always speaks to the level of sophistication of the listener

--Maximizes on visual aids & other media to describe/clarify objectives

--Effectively responds to any question on the subject

(4) --Modifies language, persuasion & emphasis depending on audience

--Shows respect, consideration & sensitivity to the response

--Clearly states facts or desired outcome

--Fields questions answering concisely & accurately

THESE STATEMENTS DESCRIBE PERSONS WHO ARE USUALLY RATED MEETING JOB STANDARDS ON COMMUNICATION SKILLS

(3) --Writes material that can be understood by non-technical readers

--Written reports are complete & require no editing by manager

--Provides timely information up & down the organization

--Gets point across-reasonable time/length; requests feedback/response to test understanding

--Deals with most questions concerning subject

--Gears appropriate terminology to audience; gives information that is complete & concise

(2) --Uses inappropriate terminology, approach or emphasis for audience

--Has difficulty understanding & answering questions

--Does not summarize/draw conclusions or achieve desired results

--Written reports require some editing by manager

THESE STATEMENTS DESCRIBE PERSONS WHO ARE USUALLY RATED UNSATISFACTORY IN COMMUNICATION SKILLS

(1) --Has difficulty speaking before a group

--Makes presentation without logical flow of thought

--Fails to listen to responses

--Often unprepared with subject matter

(0) NOT APPLICABLE OR NO OPPORTUNITY TO OBSERVE

CRITERION 2: PROBLEM-SOLVING

This criterion measures the degree to which department heads are aware of problems to be solved and know and use a variety of methods for problem resolution; also, willingness to assume risks in problem-solving issues.

THESE STATEMENTS DESCRIBE PERSONS WHO ARE USUALLY RATED OUTSTANDING ON PROBLEM-SOLVING

(5) --Anticipates problems & plans alternatives to solve them

--Seeks for & uses new, creative & innovative problem-solving techniques

--Applies team management techniques

--Calls on specially-skilled staff or others for assistance

(4) --Perceives problem & acts; considers alternatives & input from others

--Welcomes & searches for problem areas to resolve

--Willing to accept high risk if solution is best

THESE STATEMENTS DESCRIBE PERSONS WHO ARE USUALLY RATED MEETING JOB STANDARDS ON PROBLEM-SOLVING

(3) --Identifies immediate problems; searches for solutions; asks others for assistance

--Satisfactorily resolves problems <u>presented</u> or which occur in normal operations

--Considers alternatives & is willing to assume reasonable risks

--Resolves most problems that arise

(2)

THESE STATEMENTS DESCRIBE PERSONS WHO ARE USUALLY RATED UNSATISFACTORY IN PROBLEM-SOLVING

(1) --Is uninformed & has frequent "crisis" problems

--Avoids problems

--Relies on history, standard or "textbook" solutions

--Justifies preconceived solution vs. researching alternatives

(0) NOT APPLICABLE OR NO OPPORTUNITY TO OBSERVE

CRITERION 3: DECISION-MAKING

This criterion measures the ability and degree to which department heads make decisions on issues within or affecting their sphere of responsibility and authority.

THESE STATEMENTS DESCRIBE PERSONS WHO ARE USUALLY RATED OUTSTANDING IN DECISION-MAKING

(5) --95 to 100% successful results from decisions made

--Expands or saves resources as result of decisions

--Willing to invest personal effort beyond normal requirements to make sound decisions

(4) --Makes decisions willingly on difficult issues with 95% success

--Thinks issues through carefully - seeks advice of others

THESE STATEMENTS DESCRIBE PERSONS WHO ARE USUALLY RATED AS MEETING JOB STANDARDS IN DECISION-MAKING

(3) --Makes economical & timely decisions, avoiding unnecessary delays

--Consistently makes decisions that meet the department's goals & operational responsibilities

--Considers impact of decisions on others & discusses impact with those affected

--Informs manager of significant decisions prior to them becoming an issue

(2)

THESE STATEMENTS DESCRIBE PERSONS WHO ARE USUALLY RATED UNSATISFACTORY IN DECISION-MAKING

(1) --Makes decisions too quickly or too slowly

--Does not inform supervisors

--Decisions often lead to conflict, costly delays, or interrupted work schedules

--Refuses to make decisions until forced by others

(0) NOT APPLICABLE OR NO OPPORTUNITY TO OBSERVE

CRITERION 4: INTERDEPENDENCE AND COOPERATION

The ability to recognize when you need help, willingness to ask for it, knowledge of whom to ask...also willingness to accept assistance when offered or offer and provide assistance where perceived needed.

THESE STATEMENTS DESCRIBE PERSONS WHO ARE USUALLY RATED OUTSTANDING IN INTERDEPENDENCE & COOPERATION

(5) --Always willing to help others in time of need

(4) --Nearly always identifies need for & seeks outside help well in advance

--Aware of own strengths & offers those freely to peers whenever needed

--Operates as part of a team

THESE STATEMENTS DESCRIBE PERSONS WHO ARE USUALLY RATED AS MEETING JOB STANDARDS IN INTERDEPENDENCE & COOPERATION

(3) --Generally recognizes need for & seeks outside help in completing assignments

--Aware of own strengths & offers assistance most of the time to peers

--Accepts advice from others without being defensive

--Gives advice to others without attacking

(2) --Believes asking for help is a sign of weakness

THESE STATEMENTS DESCRIBE PERSONS WHO ARE USUALLY RATED UNSATISFACTORY IN INTERDEPENDENCE & COOPERATION

(1) --Acts in isolation; rarely informs others when work effort will impact them

--Seldom recognizes need for outside assistance

--Often rejects help from others

--Doesn't use abilities/strengths of superiors/peers/subordinates

(0) NOT APPLICABLE OR NO OPPORTUNITY TO OBSERVE

CRITERION 5: COST CONSCIOUSNESS

This criterion measures the degree to which department heads are conscious of total costs to the organization and seek most cost effective method for delivery of services (or administration of department).

THESE STATEMENTS DESCRIBE PERSONS WHO ARE USUALLY RATED OUTSTANDING IN COST CONSCIOUSNESS

(5) --Always stays within cost allocations

--Applies innovative or unique cost saving techniques

--Consistently looks for cost/effective procedures

(4) --Uses formal cost/benefit analysis on all projects

--Considers costs to another department in making decisions

--Questions program costs regardless of political popularity

--Sets good example of cost awareness for others by presenting a modest personal style

THESE STATEMENTS DESCRIBE PERSONS WHO ARE USUALLY RATED AS MEETING JOB STANDARDS IN COST CONSCIOUSNESS

(3) --Consistently looks for cost savings & considers costs in every decision involving expenditures

--Forecasts budget with reasonable accuracy

--Consistently keeps expenditures within budget

--Instills attitude of cost consciousness in subordinates

--Proposes only cost/effective programs

(2)

THESE STATEMENTS DESCRIBE PERSONS WHO ARE USUALLY RATED UNSATISFACTORY IN COST CONSCIOUSNESS

(1) --Strongly supports programs that are not cost/effective

--Excessive surpluses or cost overruns

--Frequently must request additional funds

--Ignores cost considerations in decisions

(0) NOT APPLICABLE OR NO OPPORTUNITY TO OBSERVE

CRITERION 6: MEETING DEADLINES AND COMMITMENTS

This criterion measures the timeliness with which reports, meetings, projects, objectives, tasks, etc., are begun and completed.

THESE STATEMENTS DESCRIBE PERSONS WHO ARE USUALLY RATED OUTSTANDING IN MEETING DEADLINES & COMMITMENTS

(5) --Always sets deadlines jointly & fulfills own responsibility

--Does not sacrifice quality of product to meet deadlines

--Completes work ahead of deadline allowing time for revision/review

--Invests personal effort beyond normal requirements to meet deadlines

(4) --Realistically sets & meets deadlines for self & subordinates

--Always on time to meetings/avoids wasting time at meetings

--Regularly produces satisfactory work ahead of schedule

--Manages time to avoid crisis situations in accomplishing work

--Renegotiates with others in advance if deadline can't be met

THESE STATEMENTS DESCRIBE PERSONS WHO ARE USUALLY RATED AS MEETING JOB STANDARDS IN MEETING DEADLINES & COMMITMENTS

(3) --Consistently meets deadlines & commitments with acceptable product

--Negotiates changes in deadlines if necessary

--Attends meetings on time without reminder

--Uses good time management practices

(2) --Submits unsatisfactory product simply to meet deadline

--Frequently misses deadlines without negotiating extensions

THESE STATEMENTS DESCRIBE PERSONS WHO ARE USUALLY RATED UNSATISFACTORY IN MEETING DEADLINES & COMMITMENTS

(1) --Often late with or forgets assignments

--Wastes own and others' time

--Frequently misses or is late to meetings

(0) NOT APPLICABLE OR NO OPPORTUNITY TO OBSERVE

CRITERION 7: INTERPERSONAL RELATIONSHIPS

The ability to build effective working relationships with others; i.e., department heads, superiors, subordinates, associates in other jurisdictions, boards, commissions, citizen groups, etc.

THESE STATEMENTS DESCRIBE PERSONS WHO ARE USUALLY RATED OUTSTANDING IN INTERPERSONAL RELATIONSHIPS

(5) --Earns & retains respect & trust of others

--Respects individual qualities of others

--Never resentful of direction by superiors

--Recognized for objectivity & leadership

--Regularly receives high honors or special appointments

(4) --Able to cooperate with all contacts while maintaining professionalism

--Confronts & mutually problem solves with others in difficult situations

--Consistently participates in & builds a team effort

THESE STATEMENTS DESCRIBE PERSONS WHO ARE USUALLY RATED AS MEETING JOB STANDARDS IN INTERPERSONAL RELATIONSHIPS

(3) --Honest & forthright in pleasant & unpleasant situations

--Avoids clannish or clique behavior

--Develops relationships of cooperation & trust with associates

--Works effectively with others to reach consensus in most situations

--Respectful of others regardless of personal values

(2)

THESE STATEMENTS DESCRIBE PERSONS WHO ARE USUALLY RATED UNSATISFACTORY IN INTERPERSONAL RELATIONSHIPS

(1) --Allows personal disputes to affect work product

--Gossips or undermines others

--Attempts to gain personal benefit from dealings with others

--Others pay no attention to his/her ideas or comments

(0) NOT APPLICABLE OR NO OPPORTUNITY TO OBSERVE

CRITERION 8: CONFIDENCE

Demonstrated self-confidence; leadership skills; ability to instill confidence in others; ability to motivate others.

THESE STATEMENTS DESCRIBE PERSONS WHO ARE USUALLY RATED OUTSTANDING IN CONFIDENCE

(5) --Highly motivated, extracts superior performance from subordinates

--Always on a high - instills a positive attitude in others

--Quickly accepts & is confident in new or unfamiliar areas

(4) --Approaches situations with "can do" attitude

--Allows subordinates substantial leeway, offering guidance when needed

--Confident when appearing before council or superiors

--Has trust of subordinates, instills pride in the organization

--No complaints received by city manager about conduct

THESE STATEMENTS DESCRIBE PERSONS WHO ARE USUALLY RATED AS MEETING JOB STANDARDS IN CONFIDENCE

(3) --Presents positive image of self, subject matter & organization

--Maintains good morale in department

--Delegates to subordinates

--Allows subordinates reasonable freedom to demonstrate competence

--Admits when doesn't know, doesn't "fake" response

(2) --Overly confident, beyond ability to perform

--Frequently needs reinforcement from superior to maintain confidence

--Continuously doubts subordinates' conclusions/results

THESE STATEMENTS DESCRIBE PERSONS WHO ARE USUALLY RATED UNSATISFACTORY IN CONFIDENCE

(1) --Displays lack of confidence in self

--Distrusts staff - fears their competency

--Vocally suspicious of others

--Unwilling to accept any element of risk

(0) NOT APPLICABLE OR NO OPPORTUNITY TO OBSERVE

CRITERION 9: PLANNING

This aspect of the job involves designing, scheduling, and implementing short and long-range plans; scheduling workload within plan; anticipating deviations from the plan.

THESE STATEMENTS DESCRIBE PERSONS WHO ARE USUALLY RATED OUTSTANDING IN PLANNING

(5) --Gives priority attention to need for planning

--Sets departmental workloads that are consistent with plans

--Almost always meets set plans

--Deviates from set schedules only in justifiable situations

(4) --Consistently formulates short & long-range (beyond one year) plans

--Achieves planned outcomes with minimum deviations

--Identifies issues/problems/goals in subordinate functional areas & develops long-range plan to resolve/achieve

THESE STATEMENTS DESCRIBE PERSONS WHO ARE USUALLY RATED AS MEETING JOB STANDARDS IN PLANNING

(3) --Establishes short & long-range program planning

--Meets priorities set by self & others

--Is able to develop plans around mission & available resources

--Can modify & update plans as circumstances change

--Doesn't wait until crisis to take action

--Develops adequate plans for future of department

(2) --Uses firefighting approach - little advance planning

--Plans without consulting other affected parties

THESE STATEMENTS DESCRIBE PERSONS WHO ARE USUALLY RATED UNSATISFACTORY IN PLANNING

(1) --Consistently operates from crisis to crisis

--Plans often not achieved

--Responds to problems after the fact

--Sticks to set schedule even if emergency requires deviation

(0) NOT APPLICABLE OR NO OPPORTUNITY TO OBSERVE

CRITERION 10: DEVELOPMENT OF STAFF

The degree to which department heads recognize staff capabilities, talents & interests, & match them to organizational requirements; also, the ability to motivate & inspire subordinates to maintain &/or upgrade technical & professional skills; the ability to evaluate employee performance.

THESE STATEMENTS DESCRIBE PERSONS WHO ARE USUALLY RATED OUTSTANDING IN DEVELOPMENT OF STAFF

(5) --Recognizes talent/puts it to work/ frequently achieves results

--Maintains exceptional level of staff morale

--Develops with employees strategies for their self-improvement

--Consistently recruits outstanding staff

--Always recognizes merit performance; awards individuals accordingly

(4) --Prepares subordinates for promotions in-house

--Delegates to staff assignments where new skills or knowledge will be needed

--High level of staff morale

THESE STATEMENTS DESCRIBE PERSONS WHO ARE USUALLY RATED AS MEETING JOB STANDARDS IN DEVELOPMENT OF STAFF

(3) --Encourages staff training & Development

--Recognizes capabilities of staff & promotes as appropriate

--Develops team effort among staff

--Moderate & consistent attention to morale

--Works with employees to solve problems of work performance

--Delegates authority & responsibility to lowest possible levels

(2) --Fails to give employee "whys" to gain perspective on work assignments

THESE STATEMENTS DESCRIBE PERSONS WHO ARE USUALLY RATED UNSATISFACTORY IN DEVELOPMENT OF STAFF

(1) --Provides no incentive or opportunity for training & development

--Allows & ignores low morale

--Hires & retains unqualified staff

(0) NOT APPLICABLE OR NO OPPORTUNITY TO OBSERVE

CRITERION 11: BUDGET PREPARATION AND MANAGEMENT

Knowledge of and ability to use established municipal budgeting processes, including management of approved (budgeted) resources.

THESE STATEMENTS DESCRIBE PERSONS WHO ARE USUALLY RATED OUTSTANDING IN BUDGET PREPARATION & MANAGEMENT

(5) --Thoroughly understands intent & mechanics of budget processes

--Uses participatory techniques in budget preparation & management

--Budget proposal reflects sensitivity to local economy/politics & city goals & objectives

--Gives high priority to proper use of city resources

(4) --Consistently completes tasks/work program with savings to budget

--Contributes to the budget process, demonstrating creativity in developing alternatives

--Develops programs with minimum assistance from budget office

--Uses program budget as management tool

THESE STATEMENTS DESCRIBE PERSONS WHO ARE USUALLY RATED AS MEETING JOB STANDARDS IN BUDGET PREPARATION & MANAGEMENT

(3) --Develops sound budgets; then stays within them

--Has basic understanding of mechanics of budget process

--Respects & abides by budgetary control policies

--Submits complete & accurate budget information within timelines

(2)

THESE STATEMENTS DESCRIBE PERSONS WHO ARE USUALLY RATED UNSATISFACTORY IN BUDGET PREPARATION & MANAGEMENT

(1) --Budgets are confusing or secretive

--Prepares budgets with no staff participation

--Spends money regardless of need

--Overspends budget allocations

--Submits incomplete & inaccurate data

(0) NOT APPLICABLE OR NO OPPORTUNITY TO OBSERVE

CRITERION 12: POLITICAL AWARENESS

This criterion measures a department head's ability to recognize and deal with issues which are potential problems for the organization.

THESE STATEMENTS DESCRIBE PERSONS WHO ARE USUALLY RATED OUTSTANDING IN POLITICAL AWARENESS

(5) --Anticipates & avoids actions which present city in unfavorable political image

--Avoids actions which would alienate elected officials or public

--Fair & truthful to press

(4) --Maintains awareness of political environment & responds pro-actively

--Alerts superiors to potential issues & develops alternative strategies

--Recommends professional & political solutions to problems

--Has awareness of current "sensitive issues" to elected officials

THESE STATEMENTS DESCRIBE PERSONS WHO ARE USUALLY RATED AS MEETING JOB STANDARDS IN POLITICAL AWARENESS

(3) --Recognizes & responds to political implications of work

--Is generally aware of politically sensitive issues

--Is aware of & tries to accommodate to ideological positions of elected officials

--Considers election process in timing projects to avoid delays

(2)

THESE STATEMENTS DESCRIBE PERSONS WHO ARE USUALLY RATED UNSATISFACTORY IN POLITICAL AWARENESS

(1) --Acts without thought to political implications

--Planning schedules don't consider potential political impacts

--Fails to support policies adopted by elected officials

--Makes public statements which compromise elected officials

(0) NOT APPLICABLE OR NO OPPORTUNITY TO OBSERVE

CRITERION 13: CONFLICT RESOLUTION

The ability to comprehend and resolve conflict (e.g., between staff-projects, public-private, council-staff, department-department, external agencies-city, etc.)

THESE STATEMENTS DESCRIBE PERSONS WHO ARE USUALLY RATED OUTSTANDING IN CONFLICT RESOLUTION

(5) --Uses conflict resolution as a positive tool for growth/goal attainment

--Highly skilled negotiator

--Can successfully act as facilitator between conflicting parties

--Consistently resolves conflicts to mutual satisfaction of parties

--Initiates conflict resolution activity early

(4) --Plans ahead for all potential problems

--Minimizes conflict through personal diplomacy

--Seldom needs outside assistance to solve problem

--Very aware of conflict indicators - takes immediate action to resolve

THESE STATEMENTS DESCRIBE PERSONS WHO ARE USUALLY RATED AS MEETING JOB STANDARDS IN CONFLICT RESOLUTION

(3) --Deals with conflict situations as they arise & resolves satisfactorily

--Effectively applies interpersonal skills to resolve issues

--Generally resolves conflicts without angering others

(2)

THESE STATEMENTS DESCRIBE PERSONS WHO ARE USUALLY RATED UNSATISFACTORY IN CONFLICT RESOLUTION

(1) --Makes no attempt to present or resolve conflicts

--Unwilling to learn conflict resolution skills

--Allows conflict to disrupt work objectives

(0) NOT APPLICABLE OR NO OPPORTUNITY TO OBSERVE

CRITERION 14: MEDIA RELATIONS

This aspect of the job involves dealing with the various media representatives; responding to requests for information; awareness of sensitive issues; use for public relations.

THESE STATEMENTS DESCRIBE PERSONS WHO ARE USUALLY RATED OUTSTANDING ON MEDIA RELATIONS

(5) --Always honest & frank with media representatives

--Avoids manipulating the press

--Gives high priority to requests for information & fully responds

--Advises other departments if aware of potential media problems in their area

(4) --Aggressively seeks cooperation of press in getting public opinion

--Keeps media informed throughout steps of projects

--Always stays within area of authority/ responsibility when dealing with media

--Presents issues positively, avoids controversial or non-factual opinions

THESE STATEMENTS DESCRIBE PERSONS WHO ARE USUALLY RATED MEETING JOB STANDARDS ON MEDIA RELATIONS

(3) --Maintains ongoing positive media relationships

--Speaks from factual information base

--Sensitive to potential public relations problems & deals with them prior to bad publicity

--Develops programs to communicate & promote elements of services

--Refers media to superior if in doubt, or on politically sensitive issues

(2) --Does not stay within area of authority/ responsibility when dealing with media

--Deals with non-factual information

--Presents opinions to media that are contrary to city policy

THESE STATEMENTS DESCRIBE PERSONS WHO ARE USUALLY RATED UNSATISFACTORY IN MEDIA RELATIONS

(1) --Refuses to speak to media

--Maintains defensive or antagonistic relationship to press

--Lies to press

--Doesn't release information unless forced

(0) NOT APPLICABLE OR NO OPPORTUNITY TO OBSERVE

CRITERION 15: TECHNICAL/PROFESSIONAL COMPETENCE

The degree to which department heads demonstrate technical knowledge & ability appropriate to the particular discipline; includes keeping abreast of state-of-the-art developments in field of responsibility.

THESE STATEMENTS DESCRIBE PERSONS WHO ARE USUALLY RATED OUTSTANDING IN TECHNICAL/PROFESSIONAL COMPETENCE

(5) --Invests considerable personal effort to increase knowledge in subject area

--Quickly accepts & welcomes assignments which offer learning opportunity

--Shares knowledge/experience with others in organization

--Has broad view of discipline & expects to be an expert

--Understands the interrelatedness of the various disciplines in city government

(4) --Able to develop viable alternatives & solve difficult problems within technical area

--Regularly attends training seminars, institutes, & conferences to stay informed of changing trends & technology

THESE STATEMENTS DESCRIBE PERSONS WHO ARE USUALLY RATED MEETING JOB STANDARDS IN TECHNICAL/PROFESSIONAL COMPETENCE

(3) --Actively participates in self-development training & state-of-the-art conferences

--Practices concepts, procedures, theories learned

--Keeps current on technical aspects of job

--Uses technical knowledge to avoid or solve problems

(2) --Ignores or avoids training opportunities

--Attends technical training opportunities at expense of work program

--Utilizes the "we've always done it this way" approach

THESE STATEMENTS DESCRIBE PERSONS WHO ARE USUALLY RATED UNSATISFACTORY IN TECHNICAL/PROFESSIONAL COMPETENCE

(1) --Out of date with technical literature

--Unfamiliar with changing trends & technology

--Makes repeated technical errors

--Doesn't attend any training opportunities

(0) NOT APPLICABLE OR NO OPPORTUNITY TO OBSERVE

Secretary

Criteria	Outstanding	Satisfactory	Unsatisfactory
Provides all typing services for unit	Typing speed exceeds 70 w.p.m. Consistently produces work which is neat and error free. Finishes assignments prior to deadline.	Typing speed within range of 50–59 w.p.m. Work contains neatly made corrections. Work may possibly be typed with accuracy, but improperly spaced on page. Produces typing assignments on time.	Typing speed is 40 w.p.m. or less. Unreliable insofar as typing errors are concerned and work must be proofed by others. Work contains obvious corrections. Unable to do other than routine typing assignments. Typing assignments frequently late.
Transcribes all dictation for unit	Transcribes dictated material with accuracy and at speed of 65 w.p.m. Corrects grammar while typing from dictation. Returns typed material in finalized form.	Transcribes dictated material accurately at speed in excess of 50 w.p.m. Completes transcription of dictated material promptly.	Transcribes drafts at a maximum speed of 45 w.p.m. Fails to transcribe dictated material by required time.
Provides "1st person" telephone and reception duties	Fields the widest range of calls. Answers technical personnel-related questions correctly. Always answers telephone and "in person" inquiries in pleasant, courteous and helpful manner.	Courteous telephone and "in person" responses. Correct transmittal of messages. Accurate referrals to other agencies. Routinely helps callers on a majority of questions.	Gives rude and/or discourteous "over the telephone" or "in person" client responses. Inability to transfer calls. Failure to communicate messages to recipients.
Maintains filing and retrieval system for departmental letters, documents and Reference Station materials	Establishes filing and cross-reference system from which materials are readily retrievable. Purges files annually.	Filing kept up-to-date. Filed materials easily retrieved. Reference Station kept current.	Filing permitted to accumulate more than two weeks. Copies misplaced prior to being filed. Materials filed incorrectly.

Is punctual and dependable	Is consistently available to assist in emergency situations.	Except for rare occasion, always punctual. Always attempts to let supervisor know when necessary to be away from office. Completes assigned tasks with very little supervision.	Frequently late for work (2 or more times per week). Abuses coffee break (2 or more times per week). Fails to carry out assigned tasks without supervision. Neglects to phone office.
Routinely performs miscellaneous office duties, including: 1. Opens and distributes mail 2. Maintains vacation/sick leave cards 3. Maintains Reference Station 4. Shares copy machine maintenance with other users. 5. Orders supplies and equipment. 6. Prepares Purchase Requisitions and Travel Vouchers.	Can be relied on to perform miscellaneous routine duties without reminders or supervision.	Needs only occasional reminder by supervisor regarding completion of routine duties.	Requires constant monitoring by supervisor to assure that duties are being completed.
Handles a range of confidential matters with discretion	Is given access to full range of confidential matters without any unauthorized disclosures.	Can be relied upon to handle a range of "normal" confidential matters without unauthorized disclosure.	On unauthorized basis often tells confidential matters to others, resulting in affected action.
Answers inquiries from callers, visitors and/or writers regarding the organization policies and procedures.	Has a full knowledge of basic University and departmental organization or can direct inquiry to the appropriate person or develop material independently. Maintains and is fully aware of formal Univ. documents on organization and personnel matters, i.e., Univ. Handbook, Operations Manual, HEPB rules, *University Week* Bulletins, etc.	Has good knowledge of basic University and department organization and can accurately refer calls to appropriate office or respond to the inquiry upon doing independent review. May ask supervisor for specific information or inquire as to where alternative sources of information are available.	Misunderstands basic University and departmental organization. Needs frequent reminders of key personnel and responsibility. Provides either wrong information or misdirects inquiries to inappropriate office.

Secretary—*Continued*

Criteria	Outstanding	Satisfactory	Unsatisfactory
Maintains effective interpersonal relations with clients, co-workers, and supervisors	Always pleasant and tactful to clients, even in adverse situations. Relates well with others working in area. Accepts criticism in a constructive manner.	Maintains good relationship with clients, co-workers, and supervisors.	Creates an atmosphere of dissension with fellow employees. Is rude to clients and/or others in working area. Generates complaints about personal "style"

Budget Coordinator A

Criteria	Outstanding	Satisfactory	Unsatisfactory
Prepares all appointment and payroll documents for faculty, staff, and students.	Prepares documents and forms promptly, accurately, and neatly. Uses own initiative without supervision gathering materials needed. Meets all deadlines on or before deadline date.	Prepares documents and forms accurately and neatly. Submits material by deadline.	Prepares documents and forms without checking for accuracy. Occasionally misses deadline.
Maintains personnel and grant files.	Prepares files immediately. Keeps files updated at all times. Able to give information immediately when asked.	Prepares files when time permits (within a few days). Able to produce information same day asked.	Filing permitted to accumulate for more than a week. Material filed incorrectly. Unable to give information from files.
Operates and/or supervises the operation of the computer bookkeeping system.	Always maintains updated budget summary (including salary register) showing expenditures, encumbrances and projected costs for each grant, contract, or budget.	Able to produce updated budget summary with one day's notice.	Fails to maintain budget summaries which are accurate and up-to-date.
Control expenditures within budget limitations.	Always able to maintain control of expenditures to keep within budget limitations; advises supervisor in advance of potential problems and provides alternatives.	Able to maintain control of expenditures. Implements procedures of the organization to control expenditures within budget limitations.	Fails to maintain control of expenditures to keep within budget limitations. Fails to inform supervisor of status and developing problems.
Travel procedures. Advises and assists faculty with regards to policies and procedures related to specific travel. Prepares all travel documents.	Travel forms are completed accurately with no errors. Can assist faculty in development of itinerary. Prepares and maintains complete travel records for faculty and guest seminar speakers.	Small percentage of forms are in error and returned for corrections. General knowledge of policy changes. All necessary receipts are submitted. Discuss with faculty the rules that would apply to specific travel, i.e., high cost areas, receipts necessary for reimbursement, and information on travel advances.	Forms submitted are returned for frequent revisions. Correct signatures are not obtained. Forms are not submitted by particular deadline. Forms are prepared in the face of recognized omissions.

Budget Coordinator A—*Continued*

Criteria	*Outstanding*	*Satisfactory*	*Unsatisfactory*
Working relationship and coordination of job tasks.	Knows and performs all duties of the accounting office and initiates action. Recommends improvements to existing procedures. Works closely with supervisor and co-worker. Performs all aspects of budget office work including those not specifically assigned to one or the other budget coordinator.	Has basic knowledge of and performs accounting duties as assigned. Notifies supervisor and co-worker of present job status and problems. Has ability to report on status of tasks handled by other budget coordinator as well as her own.	Has limited knowledge of accounting duties to be performed. Fails to communicate job status with supervisor and co-worker. Performs duties only as assigned.
Has and applies knowledge of University and grant and contract procedures and regulations; i.e., Grant Information Memoranda and Grants Policy Statement.	Understands and applies knowledge of University and grant/contract procedures and regulations; takes initiative to find answers on regulations.	Some knowledge of University and grant/contract regulations and procedures. Utilizes references and resources to obtain needed information.	Does not have knowledge of procedures and regulations; never takes the initiative to seek the answer.
Prepare cost projections for grant proposals or budgets.	Prepares budget projections for grant and contract proposals or state budgets with minimum assistance from principal investigator/supervisor.	Helps prepare budget for grant and contract proposals or state budgets with assistance from principal investigator/supervisor.	Unable to help principal investigator/supervisor prepare budget for grant and contract proposals or state budgets.
Communications—oral and written.	Makes special efforts to answer inquiries. Information provided is always accurate and complete.	Information is communicated clearly and accurately. Written communications are promptly answered and answers are clear and complete. Telephone messages are correctly routed and recorded.	Communicates wrong information. Letters are vague. Discourteous to people. Delays answering inquiries.

Supervisory skills.	Knows the purchasing assistant's work and responsibilities and gives her a chance to use own initiative and to be responsible for job. Always available to talk to her. Disciplines, when necessary, with authority in non-abrasive manner. Ability to sense when discipline is necessary.	Knows the purchasing assistant's work. Supervises some work and responsibilities. Is available to talk to her when time permits. Disciplines when necessary.	Does not know purchasing assistant's work completely. Does not check that work and responsibilities are being carried out. Does not discipline unless absolutely necessary. Often uses wrong tone or approach.
Interviews and makes recommendations to administration in the hiring of certain staff.	Interviews applicant carefully and thoroughly. Gives applicant time to explain qualifications and experience. Explains thoroughly all elements of job. Is receptive to questions of applicant. Informs administration or supervisor promptly of evaluation of candidate. Shares reference checking responsibility.	Interviews applicant carefully and thoroughly. Explains the work and responsibilities of position. Informs administration or supervisor of evaluation of candidate. Shares reference checking responsibility.	Interviews applicant superficially. Has others explain work and responsibilities of position. Does not inform administration or supervisor promptly of evaluation of candidate. Relies on the decision of others. Does not provide careful, thorough analysis of candidate to administration or supervisor.
Ability to work under tight time pressures.	Works under tight time schedules with speed, accuracy, and efficiency. Never gets upset when some emergency situation arises which creates a necessity for change in priorities.	Adapts easily to emergency situations. Produces error-free work in required time.	Unable to work under pressure in emergency situations. Can not produce error-free work when working in a tight time frame.
Ability to organize and produce work in orderly manner.	Uses own initiative to determine which jobs are priority items. Keeps work flowing smooth, even when working for two or more people. Organizes work and produces finished product with speed, accuracy and efficiency.	Determines priorities with some assistance. Except for rare occasion is able to keep work flowing smoothly when working on two or more projects. Organizes and produces work assignments on time. Informs supervisor of status of priority items.	Unable to recognize priority job. Does not complete work in required time. Fails to inform supervisor of status of projects.

Budget Coordinator A—*Continued*

Criteria	Outstanding	Satisfactory	Unsatisfactory
Is punctual and dependable.	Is consistently available to assist in emergency situations, meet with staff, faculty, students, and supervisor. Consistently completes all tasks on time.	Except for rare occasion, is always punctual. Always attempts to let supervisor know when necessary to be away from office. Completes tasks.	Frequently late for work. Abuses coffee break. Fails to carry out assigned tasks without supervision.

Performance Evaluation Criteria for Animal Technician 1 (with performance levels)

Criteria	Outstanding	Satisfactory	Unsatisfactory
Attendance	has perfect attendance except for using vacation time properly authorized.	uses no more leave time than has been accrued. averages no more than six days sick leave per year.	takes 16 hours or more unscheduled leave per month during a three-month period.
Punctuality	always arrives a little early and is ready to start working shortly before the scheduled time.	arrives on time for work and is not late more than 10 minutes (not exceeding three days per month). stays until end of scheduled work period.	arrives more than 10 minutes late six times or more per month. leaves before the end of the scheduled work period frequently without authorization.
*Ability to follow instructions (oral, written, and departmental policies)	follows instructions without assistance in interpretation. recognizes flaws in instructions. never needs to be told something more than once.	knows where to look for needed instructions. follows daily instructions accurately 100% of time. follows special instructions accurately 85% of time.	needs to be reminded often of instructions. does not follow instructions accurately.
Machine operation and maintenance	detects subtle changes in machine function and operation. has ability to repair machine and maintain at peak performance level.	knows normal machine functions; reports abnormal function to appropriate person. operates machine correctly; e.g., has proper time settings, uses appropriate chemical for type of cleaning. is aware of personal limitations in ability to repair or alter any machine.	does not operate machine properly. abuses machine. does not notice and/or report abnormal machine function.

*It is the opinion of the committee that the levels of performance should be adjusted on these criteria for animal technicians 2 and 3; otherwise they apply to all three classifications as listed. Additional criteria are listed separately for the higher classifications.

Performance Evaluation Criteria for Animal Technician 1—*Continued* (with performance levels)

Criteria	Outstanding	Satisfactory	Unsatisfactory
Use of supplies, materials (disinfectants, uniforms, gloves, masks, cleaning agents, etc.)	supplies and materials always on hand and ready for use in assigned areas. has innovative ideas for better ways of using supplies.	uses proper agents with particular species. uses correct disinfectant and cleaner in assigned areas. makes efficient use of materials. knows when to replace items. wears clean uniform daily. normally has supplies and materials on hand in assigned areas.	uses improper combinations of cleaning/disinfecting agents. often wears dirty uniform.
*Animal care (feeding, watering, cleaning of cages)	changes cages when needed beyond established schedule. makes innovative suggestions for improving procedures.	adheres to prescribed schedules. feeds, waters appropriate amounts and kinds. changes flooded cages immediately.	misses scheduled feedings and waterings and cleaning schedules. puts newly arrived animals in dirty cages. returns animals to other than their own cages. mixes water bottles and feeders among animals.
Cleaning and maintaining assigned rooms	performs special needed cleanings beyond schedule. always maintains a neat and orderly room appearance, as well as clean.	makes sure that all animals are identified properly. checks automatic watering systems, maintains in good order; reports problems to designated person. keeps rooms properly stocked. uses drains and sinks correctly. cleans room in prescribed order.	ignores physical plant problems. does not always clean room. overstocks (hoards) supplies.

Criterion	(High)	(Middle)	(Low)
*Observation and reporting of animals for health and behavior patterns, problems, changes	picks up subtle signs of patterns, problems, and changes.	observes all animals daily. notes whether animals are eating, not eating, not drinking, abnormal defecation, urination, and lethargic signs. observes and reports dead animals. makes complete and accurate reporting of what was observed.	misses daily observations. reports observations inaccurately. does not report observations at all.
*Record maintenance (per diem, preventive health cage cards, time records special requests, etc.)	maintains absolutely accurate, neat, and complete records. makes suggestions for methods of improving record keeping.	completes the records, giving all information requested on form. knows which records are for what purpose. provides information with at least 90% degree of accuracy.	keeps inaccurate records. does not have required records in room, or cage cards on cage.
Handling emergency work situations	always willing to do other work, completing the tasks satisfactorily.	willing to do other work with proper completion, not leaving own work unless agreed upon at least two-thirds of the time. performs weekend/holiday work on rotating schedule when requested.	never is willing to do other (more) work when requested. is willing to do extra work, but never completes task in satisfactory manner.
*Effective interaction with coworkers, investigators	can work with many different people. knows where proper loyalty lies. effectively communicates departmental policies to outsiders. cleans up after oneself; does not create extra work for others (particularly in non-work areas).	willing to go "extra mile" in effort. willing to work with co-workers even though you may not like them personally. willing to put up with investigators and their "peculiarities."	"giving away the company store" (offering services with no recharge; changing policies for some customers). swearing at investigators, supervisors and co-workers. goofing off with co-workers.

*It is the opinion of the committee that the levels of performance should be adjusted on these criteria for animal technicians 2 and 3; otherwise they apply to all three classifications as listed. Additional criteria are listed separately for the higher classifications.

Performance Evaluation Criteria for Animal Technician 1—*Continued*
(with performance levels)

Criteria	Outstanding	Satisfactory	Unsatisfactory
Use of working time	can repeatedly adjust time to allow for fluctuations in work load. makes suggestions for better use of working time.	completes assigned daily tasks satisfactorily. asks appropriate person for help in work and for answers to questions; does not waste time of self and others by going to wrong people for help. uses time efficiently in gathering needed supplies, etc.; does not make unnecessary trips from one area to another.	fails to complete reasonable assigned daily tasks. wastes own and co-workers' time by talking too much, etc. excessive "spinning of wheels".

Performance Evaluation Criteria for Animal Technician 2

Criteria	Outstanding	Satisfactory	Unsatisfactory
All those listed for Animal Technician 1	Same as listed previously, except for those marked with an (*).		
Working independently	prioritize work successfully.	can perform all Animal Technician 1 duties independently. knows the limits of technical competence, judgment, responsibility, etc.	cannot perform duties without repeated instructions.
Technical performance	specifics should be worked out by individual departments since the kinds of work performed vary considerably.		

Additional Criteria for Animal Technician 3

Criteria	Outstanding	Satisfactory	Unsatisfactory
Lead performance	increases the effectiveness and efficiency of the unit. motivates other workers.	effectively interacts with others. effectively delegates work. maintains own work load.	does not have ability to communicate well. shows favoritism in work assignments, etc. overlooks problems, poor performance, etc. in employee he/she is leading.
Working independently (repeat of previously listed criteria at Tech 2 level)	helps out independently where help is needed.	prioritizes work successfully. performs Animal Technician 2 duties independently.	does not know departmental policy. needs instruction to carry out basic tasks.
Assisting investigators in determining animal care needs	should be determined according to needs of individual departments.		

Administrative Assistant B

Criteria	Outstanding	Satisfactory	Unsatisfactory
Prepares all appointment and payroll documents for faculty, staff and students	Prepares documents and forms promptly, accurately, and neatly. Uses own initiative without supervision gathering materials needed. Meets all deadlines on or before deadline date.	Prepares documents and forms accurately and neatly. Submits material by deadline.	Prepares documents and forms without checking for accuracy. Occasionally misses deadline.
Maintains filing system for all faculty, staff and students, and Reference Station materials.	Prepares files for employees immediately. Keeps files updated at all times. Able to give information immediately when asked. Files Reference Station corrections immediately and knows most of the procedures and policies.	Prepares files for employees when time permits (within a few days). Files material and Reference Station corrections when time permits. Able to produce information same day asked.	Filing permitted to accumulate for more than a week. Materials filed incorrectly. Unable to give information from files.
Prepares time schedules and curriculum changes.	Works closely with time schedule and curriculum committees. Checks that all scheduling and curriculum changes are accurate. Uses own initiative without supervision gathering scheduling and curriculum information. Submits on or before deadline.	Enters accurately all information on time schedule sheets and curriculum changes. Submits by deadline.	Enters schedule and curriculum information without checking. Waits until last minute to do entries and frequently misses deadline.
Student information	Knows all aspects of student advising offices. Knows procedures and policies to answer questions without referring student elsewhere. Spends some time talking to students pleasantly and courteously.	Answers student questions when able. Refers them to proper offices for answers. Answers pleasantly and courteously.	Lets staff answer student questions. Has little or no contact with students. Frequently is not polite or pleasant to students.

Supervises classified staff.	Knows each staff position's work and responsibilities. Gives staff a chance to use own initiative and to be responsible for job. Always available to talk to staff. Disciplines when necessary with authority in nonabrasive manner. Ability to sense when discipline is necessary.	Knows each staff position. Supervises some work and responsibilities. Is available to talk to staff when time permits. Disciplines when necessary.	Does not know each staff position completely. Does not check that work and responsibilities are being carried out. Does not discipline unless absolutely necessary. Often uses wrong tone or approach.
Hiring staff.	Interviews applicant carefully and thoroughly. Gives applicant time to explain qualifications and experiences. Explains thoroughly all elements of job. Uses own initiative if applicant should be interviewed by another person. Informs applicant promptly when decision is made.	Interviews applicant carefully and thoroughly. Explains the work and responsibilities of position. Has other staff or faculty interview applicant. Informs applicant promptly of decision.	Interviews applicant superficially. Has staff member explain work and responsibilities of position. Has staff members interview applicant. Does not notify promptly. Waits decision of others.
Provides information for departmental budget, reports and any other data compilations.	Has record-keeping system for immediate access to financial, enrollment, and other data. Takes the initiative without supervision to research data for all reports. Writes some reports and anticipates deadlines and prepares report well in advance.	Has record-keeping system for ready access to financial, enrollment and other data. Assists supervisor in preparing and writing reports. Prepares reports in time for deadlines.	Looks up data when asked. Types reports for supervisor. Frequently misses deadline.
Handles a range of confidential matters with discretion.	Is given access to full range of confidential matters such as contemplated salary increases, promotions, etc., without any unauthorized disclosures.	Can be relied upon to handle a range of "normal" confidential matters without unauthorized disclosures.	On unauthorized basis provides or tells confidential matters to others, resulting in hurt to an employee or damage to program.
Maintains effective interpersonal relations with clients, co-workers and supervisor.	Always pleasant and tactful to clients, even in adverse situations. Relates well with others working in department. Accepts criticism in a constructive manner. Maintains good working relationship with supervisor.	Maintains good relationship with clients, co-workers and supervisor.	Creates an atmosphere of dissension with fellow employees. Is rude to clients and/or others in department.

Administrative Assistant B—Continued

Criteria	Outstanding	Satisfactory	Unsatisfactory
Ability to work under tight time pressures.	Works under tight time schedules with speed, accuracy, and efficiency. Never gets upset when some emergency situation arises which creates a necessity for change in priorities.	Adapts easily to emergency situations. Produces error-free work in required time.	Unable to work under pressure in emergency situations. Cannot produce error-free work when working in a tight time frame.
Ability to organize and produce work in orderly manner.	Uses own initiative to determine which jobs are priority items. Keeps work flow smooth, even when working for two or more people. Organizes work and produces finished product with speed, accuracy and efficiency.	Determines priorities with some assistance. Except for rare occasion is able to keep work flow smooth when working for two or more people. Organizes and produces work assignments on time.	Unable to recognize priority job. Does not complete work in required time.
Is punctual and dependable.	Is consistently available to assist in emergency situations, meet with staff, faculty, students and supervisor. Consistently completes all tasks on time.	Except for rare occasion, always punctual. Always attempts to let supervisor know when necessary to be away from office. Completes tasks.	Frequently late for work. Abuses coffee break. Fails to carry out assigned tasks without supervision.

SENIOR OPERATOR
EMPLOYEE PERFORMANCE EVALUATION

EMPLOYEE'S NAME: _____

RATER'S NAME: _____

PERIOD COVERED: _____ TO: _____

JOB TITLE: _____

NUMBER OF YEARS/MONTHS IN PRESENT POSITION: _____

The performance evaluation is divided into six (6) parts: Part I is comprised of the rating scales identified by the incumbents and their supervisors as important aspects of their jobs; Parts II-VI provide for a narrative description of an employee's performance and for future planning.

Part I—Rating Levels

The purpose of the rating levels is to provide you with an objective way of evaluating your employee's performance. There are six major criteria or tasks: Safety, Coordinating Work (Supervising), Professional Attitude Toward Work, Operations, Public Relations, and Interpretation of Plant Machinery. The statements under each criterion describe the kinds of behaviors or activities you might observe in an employee doing a poor, good, or outstanding job and serve as anchor points.

Before rating an employee on a criterion, read through all the statements. Then place a check mark next to each of the statements that describe the employee's behavior or activity as you have observed it. Keep in mind that these statements assume the behavior described occurred *consistently* throughout the rating period. Do not place any marks beside items which the employee *did not* do, or which you did not personally observe him/her doing.

After checking the individual statements, then check the level of the employee's performance for that criterion. An employee's behavior for a certain criterion may not all be at the one performance level. However, you should be able to arrive at a summary judgment. Keep in mind also that if you rate an employee at the top performance level (exceeding job standards), it is assumed that he/she will have demonstrated the kinds of behavior stated in the level below.

When you have completed the ratings on each criterion, you are through with Part I. *Do not* attempt to determine an overall or average rating across all criteria for an employee at this time. Performance on each criterion should be examined and evaluated separately.

Parts II-VI—Narrative

Parts II-IV allow you, the supervisor and the employee, an opportunity to emphasize, expand, or clarify the ratings made in Part I and to develop performance objectives for the next rating period. At Part V, check one of two boxes provided to indicate the employee's overall performance level and your intention to review that performance in the future.

PERFORMANCE LEVELS

Three performance levels are used in this evaluation. They are as follows:

- Examples of behavior which consistently exceed job standards—performance which is beyond what's expected.
- Examples of behavior that meet job standards—consistently good, competent, proficient performance. Employees rated at this level would be considered capable of taking on additional responsibilities or a higher position requiring skill in this criterion.
- Examples of behavior that are consistently below job standards—performance that needs improvement or is unacceptable.

SAFETY

Overall Rating

☐ Performance exceeds job standards—is beyond what is expected.

☐ Consistently good, competent, and proficient in meeting job standards.

☐ Does not meet job standards consistently. Performance in need of improvement.

☐ Not applicable or no opportunity to observe.

Examples of Behavior

_____ Seeks ways to improve safe work procedures and conditions.

_____ Commends employees for outstanding safety performance.

_____ Discusses safety record with crew frequently.

_____ Asks employees for ideas on how to improve safety performance.

_____ Stresses shop safety record and housekeeping with new employees.

_____ Keeps employees informed of new safety and housekeeping requirements.

_____ Trains and corrects employees in use of good safety habits.

_____ Sets a good example for employees by using proper safety techniques.

_____ Maintains facility/equipment at required level.

_____ Attends all required safety meetings.

_____ Investigates and corrects possible safety problems in his/her area.

_____ Is careless in use of equipment, resulting in breakdowns and loss of time.

_____ Enforces regulations only when expects visit from state or federal authorities.

_____ Sort of lets things take their own course; does very little toward a positive approach to accident prevention.

_____ Doesn't follow up on safety suggestions from crew.

_____ Doesn't hold regular safety sessions with crew.

_____ Ignores safety violations.

COORDINATING WORK
(SUPERVISING)

Overall Rating

☐ Performance exceeds job standards—is beyond what is expected.

Examples of Behavior

_____ Assumes responsibility for a plant and makes decisions in the absence of a supervisor when designated.

_____ Helps employees work out problems between themselves.

_____ Treats employees impartially.

_____ Gains respect of other employees.

_____ Works well with other people and sections to solve problems.

_____ Checks to see how work is progressing.

_____ Explains new procedures to subordinates clearly.

_____ Determines when to make decisions independently and when to refer situations to higher authority.

☐ Consistently good, competent, and proficient in meeting job standards.

_____ Adheres to, checks on and applies policies, personnel rules and regulations and labor agreements.

_____ Efficiently uses time, material and human resources to accomplish tasks.

_____ Responds to machinery problems by calling correct source for help.

_____ Retrains employees when necessary.

_____ Conducts objective evaluations of employees.

_____ Holds monthly safety meetings with employees and submits reports.

_____ Decides best employee to assign task to, based on employee's skills and abilities.

_____ Trains new operators and utility workers.

_____ Keeps other people informed of progress and important happenings.

_____ Follows up after training to make sure employee is performing tasks correctly.

_____ Plans and schedules routine work.

☐ Does not meet job standards consistently. Performance in need of improvement.

_____ Requires supervisor's or other's approval before making any decisions.

_____ Does not inform people of work progress or important happenings.

_____ Assigns work without regard to employee's skills and abilities.

_____ Gives incomplete or unclear instructions to subordinates.

_____ Leaves station without notifying others of whereabouts.

☐ Not applicable or no opportunity to observe.

PROFESSIONAL ATTITUDE TOWARD WORK

Overall Rating *Examples of Behavior*

☐ Performance exceeds job standards—is beyond what is expected.

_____ Suggests new and improved work methods.
_____ Politely accepts unsolicited, informal advice and comments from a number of people other than his/her supervisor.
_____ Takes classes and reads information to keep up on field on own time.
_____ Sees what needs to be done and accomplishes work without being asked.

☐ Consistently good, competent, and proficient in meeting job standards.

_____ Willingly accepts criticism and evaluations from others.
_____ Avoids abusing sick leave.
_____ Does repetitive work willingly.
_____ Calls in an hour in advance if unable to come to work.
_____ Works shifts and holidays as requested.
_____ Comes to work on time.
_____ Comes to work every day unless on vacation or on legitimate sick leave.
_____ Works overtime in an emergency.

☐ Does not meet job standards consistently. Performance in need of improvement.

_____ Waits to be told what to do next.
_____ Often complains and expresses negativism before learning all facts of situation.
_____ Waits until last minute to start or complete work.
_____ Knowingly waits for someone else to discover work mistakes before correcting.
_____ Displays little concern with own mistakes.
_____ Is late without acceptable excuse.
_____ Misses work without acceptable reason.

☐ Not applicable or no opportunity to observe.

OPERATIONS

Overall Rating

☐ Performance exceeds job standards—is beyond what is expected.

☐ Consistently good, competent, and proficient in meeting job standards.

☐ Does not meet job standards consistently. Performance in need of improvement.

☐ Not applicable or no opportunity to observe.

Examples of Behavior

_____
_____

_____ Anticipates effects of specific operational activities on other parts of the process.

_____ Deals with problems when there is no set procedure for handling.

_____ Shifts smoothly to new tasks when priorities change.

_____ Works with little or no supervision in the area of equipment or process maintenance and adjustment.

_____ Keeps others informed of equipment/process status.

_____ Uses proper type of pump for proper application.

_____ Applies procedures according to plant manuals or instructions.

_____ Is alert to operational problems, identifies causes and takes corrective action, such as: aeration blowers, grit cyclones, emergency power, CATAD.

_____ Does not identify or respond correctly to operational problems such as: aeration blowers, grit cyclones, emergency power, CATAD.

_____ Takes more time than expected to finish work.

_____ Keeps incomplete and/or inaccurate records or reports.

_____ Does not apply or follow correct procedures to restore plant operation after plant shutdown.

_____ Has physical limitations which prevent performance of job such as: unable to climb stairs, to lift heavy objects, to drive safely.

PUBLIC RELATIONS

Overall Rating

☐ Performance exceeds job standards—is beyond what is expected.

☐ Consistently good, competent, and proficient in meeting job standards.

Examples of Behavior

_____ Personally follows through and calls back on private citizens' concerns about lost items, etc.

_____ Presents favorable image to the public at all times when on the job.

_____ Makes reports of complaints.

_____ Follows through on complaints by taking appropriate action.

_____ Calms angry people who call or come by to complain about Company activities.

_____ Represents Company in a dignified manner when dealing with the public.

_____ Provides appropriate information to public about plant operation.

_____ Interacts courteously with the public.

_____ Conducts tours in professional manner.

☐ Does not meet job standards consistently. Performance in need of improvement.

_____ Presents unfavorable image of Company to the public.

_____ Criticizes Company to the public.

_____ Is rude to the public.

_____ Provides misinformation to people when doesn't know the answers to the questions asked.

☐ Not applicable or no opportunity to observe.

INTERPRETATION OF PLANT MACHINERY

Overall Rating

☐ Performance exceeds job standards—is beyond what is expected.

☐ Consistently good, competent, and proficient in meeting job standards.

Examples of Behavior

_____ Is so familiar with machinery as to detect and note the slightest indicators of future trouble.

_____ Detects and notes abnormal operating conditions of machinery.

_____ Reads and correctly interprets dials, indicators, controllers, charts.

_____ Determines if a grinder is plugged by the pattern of LP water on the strip chart and/or sump level indicator, and unplugs it.

_____ Recognizes normal packing function.

_____ Determines if machinery problem is electrical or mechanical before calling for help.

_____ Correctly performs and interprets lab tests and takes corrective action according to circumstances.

_____ Determines if Cl_2 analyzers are operating normally, runs check on problems and takes corrective action.

_____ Refers to and interprets engineering drawings correctly.

_____ Recognizes and correctly reacts to unusual power usages.

☐ Does not meet job standards consistently. Performance in need of improvement.

_____ Misinterprets dials, indicators, controllers and charts.

_____ Ignores early warning signals of equipment malfunction until system failure requires action.

☐ Not applicable or no opportunity to observe.

Part II—Performance Development

In this section list those specific areas in which the employee has performed well. Include any outstanding examples of behavior that occurred during the rating period. Be sure to include accomplishments of objectives agreed to at last appraisal. Attach any interim documentation (logs, memos) of critical incidents.

_____
_____
_____
_____
_____

Part III—Performance Development

In this section list those specific areas (from Part I) in which the employee needs to improve. Be sure to include objectives *not met* from last appraisal. Attach any interim documentation (i.e., logs, memos) of critical incidents.

_____
_____
_____
_____
_____
_____

Part IV—Performance Objectives

In this section list specific objectives to improve performance during the next review period and actions to be taken to accomplish them. Be sure to address those areas listed in Part III.

Objective	Action to be Taken	Person to take Action

Part V—General Comments

In this section list any pertinent facts that should be known about the employee. For example, long illness or absence during rating period, any special talents or skills that the employee has which may be used to advantage in other activities or positions, and any recommendations you have, etc.

_____
_____
_____
_____

☐ Employee is performing satisfactorily and will be evaluated at the next regular performance evaluation session.

☐ Employee will be evaluated in _____ months because of unsatisfactory performance in following areas:

_____
_____

Part VI—Employee Comments

In this section the employee should state any areas of concern or disagreement with his/her appraisal.

_____
_____
_____
_____

RATER'S SIGNATURE: _____ _____
　　　　　　　　　　　　　　　　　　　　　　　　　　　　　　　　date

EMPLOYEE'S SIGNATURE: _____ _____
Your signature does not necessarily mean that you agree with the ratings.　date

I WOULD LIKE TO DISCUSS THIS REPORT OR OTHER MATTERS WITH SOMEONE OTHER THAN MY RATING SUPERVISOR.

　　　　　　　　　　　　　　　　　　　　　　　　　　_____　_____
　　　　　　　　　　　　　　　　　　　　　　　　　　　YES　　　NO

REVIEWER'S SIGNATURE: _____ _____
　　　　　　　　　　　　　　　　　　　　　　　　　　　　　　　　date

Reviewer's Comments: _____
_____
_____

EMPLOYEE PERFORMANCE EVALUATION
SCHEDULE MAKERS

EMPLOYEE'S NAME: _____

RATER'S NAME: _____

PERIOD COVERED: _____ TO: _____

JOB TITLE: _____

NUMBER OF YEARS/MONTHS IN PRESENT POSITION: _____

This performance evaluation is divided into six (6) parts: Part I is comprised of the rating scales identified by the incumbents and their supervisors as important aspects of their jobs; Parts II-VI provide for a narrative description of an employee's performance and for future planning.

Part I—Rating Scales

The purpose of the rating scales is to provide you with an objective way of evaluating your employee's performance. There are seven major criteria or tasks: Schedule Writing, Interpreting Oral and Written Instructions, Following Through, Meeting Deadlines, Working Under Pressure, Working Without Supervision, and Getting Along With Others. The statements under each criterion describe the kinds of behaviors or activities you might observe in an employee doing a poor, good, or outstanding job and serve as anchor points.

Before rating an employee on a criterion, read through all the statements. Then place a check mark next to each of the statements that describe the employee's behavior or activity as you have observed it. Keep in mind that these statements assume the behavior described occurred consistently throughout the rating period. Do not place any marks beside items which the employee *did not* do, or which you did not personally observe him/her doing.

After checking the individual statements, then check the level of the employee's performance for that criterion. An employee's behavior for a certain criterion may not all be at the one performance level. However, you should be able to arrive at a summary judgment. Keep in mind also that if you rate an employee at the top performance level (exceeding job standards), it is assumed that he/she will have demonstrated the kinds of behavior stated in the level below.

When you have completed the ratings on each criterion, you are through with Part I. *Do not* attempt to determine an overall or average rating across all criteria for an employee at this time. Performance on each criterion should be examined and evaluated separately.

Part II-VI—Narrative

Parts II-VI allow you, the supervisor and the employee, an opportunity to emphasize, expand, or clarify the ratings made in part I and to develop performance objectives for the next rating period. In Part V, check one of two boxes provided to indicate the employee's overall performance level and your intention to review that performance in the future.

PERFORMANCE LEVELS

Three performance levels are used in this evaluation. They are as follows:

- Examples of behavior which consistently exceeds job standards—performance which goes beyond what is expected.

- Examples of behavior which meet job standards—*consistently good, competent, and proficient* performance. Employees rated at this level would be considered capable of taking on additional responsibilities or a higher position requiring skill in this criterion.

- Examples of behavior which are consistently below job standards—performance that needs improvement or is unacceptable.

SCHEDULE WRITING

Overall Rating　　　　　　　　　　　　　　　　*Examples of Behavior*

☐ Performance exceeds job standards—is beyond what is expected.

　　_____ Solves schedule problems without asking for help from supervisory personnel.

　　_____ Saves money by writing schedules which save platform hours and/or coaches.

　　_____ Seldom makes computer errors, less than five per schedule.

　　_____ Checks all information pertaining to the schedule package including monitors' information and notifies supervisory personnel immediately if there are problems.

☐ Consistently good, competent, and proficient in meeting job standards.

　　_____ Sets service needs to correspond with start/quit times, although may occasionally need to be reminded by supervisory personnel.

　　_____ Utilizes proper headway, deadhead and running times when writing a schedule.

　　_____ Meets budget constraints in a schedule and utilizes the assigned number of coaches and hours.

　　_____ Incorporates information provided by the monitors in writing a schedule.

　　_____ Fills in computer forms correctly, less than ten errors per schedule.

☐ Does not meet job standards consistently. Performance in need of improvement.

　　_____ Fails to recognize problems in schedule packages or, when does notice the problem, does not notify appropriate supervisory personnel.

　　_____ Schedule times do not meet service needs.

　　_____ Never checks any information pertaining to the schedule package.

　　_____ Disregards budget constraints; may develop schedules that need extra hours or coaches.

　　_____ Needs to be constantly reminded to utilize proper headway, deadhead and running times in writing a schedule.

☐ Not applicable or no opportunity to observe.

INTERPRETING ORAL AND WRITTEN INSTRUCTIONS

Overall Rating *Examples of Behavior*

☐ Performance exceeds job standards—is beyond what is expected.

_____ Reviews instructions completely, before asking questions, so that he/she is able to get all their questions answered the first time.

_____ Seldom asks questions on minor routine instructions, but makes it a point to get clarification if necessary on more complex or detailed instructions.

_____ Makes suggestions on instructions as to how they could be improved.

☐ Consistently good, competent, and proficient in meeting job standards.

_____ Usually reviews instructions before asking any questions.

_____ Makes notes on oral instructions when necessary to insure that the instructions are carried out properly.

_____ When in doubt about instructions, asks questions.

☐ Does not meet job standards consistently. Performance in need of improvement.

_____ Takes instructions but does not ask for any help or clarification if he/she has questions.

_____ Forgets to make notes on oral instruction or often forgets parts of instructions resulting in errors.

_____ Does not review complete instructions before asking questions.

☐ Not applicable or no opportunity to observe.

FOLLOWING THROUGH

Overall Rating *Examples of Behavior*

☐ Performance exceeds job standards—is beyond what is expected.

_____ Checks for proper "Y" routes and "indicates".
_____ Checks with other Schedule Makers to insure that trips can be connected when necessary.
_____ Makes several checks with supervisory personnel during schedule writing to make sure that necessary revisions are incorporated.
_____ Reviews completed schedules to make sure that they have incorporated the most recent information available.
_____ Makes sure that all necessary forms are prepared upon completion of the schedule (i.e. headway charts, timetables, etc.).

☐ Consistently good, competent and proficient in meeting job standards.

_____ Checks deviations from regular schedules.
_____ Checks school routes for proper deadhead times.
_____ Includes correct maps for all school routes.
_____ Checks schedule(s) for foreign trips.
_____ Checks for schedule meets on other routes.
_____ Keeps supervisory personnel informed regarding work progress.

☐ Does not meet job standards consistently. Performance in need of improvement.

_____ Fails to check "Y" routes, school trips, deviations from regular schedules, deadhead times, and schedule meets.
_____ Does not keep supervisory personnel informed of work progress.
_____ Forgets to check with other Schedule Makers regarding foreign trip availability; just assumes that completed schedules will have hook-ups available.
_____ Fails to review completed schedule prior to submittal to supervisory personnel.

☐ Not applicable or no opportunity to observe.

MEETING DEADLINES

Overall Rating

☐ Performance exceeds job standards—is beyond what is expected.

☐ Consistently good, competent, and proficient in meeting job standards.

☐ Does not meet job standards consistently. Performance in need of improvement.

☐ Not applicable or no opportunity to observe.

Examples of Behavior

_____ Consistently exceeds/beats all deadlines.

_____ Continually checks with supervisory personnel to make sure that any revisions to a schedule can be incorporated within the necessary deadlines.

_____ When a scheduled deadline is affected by the work of another employee, he/she will make sure that supervisory personnel are notified so that deadlines can be adjusted.

_____ Makes recommendations to set up effective work priorities so that scheduled deadlines can be adjusted.

_____ Meets all deadlines.

_____ Coordinates workload with supervisory personnel to set up work priorities.

_____ Continually makes progress checks to insure that necessary deadlines are being met.

_____ When revisions are necessary, makes an effort to meet deadlines.

_____ Fails to meet deadlines.

_____ Forgets to make progress checks so falls behind work schedules frequently.

_____ Neglects to include revisions into schedules and has to go back and make corrections after work deadlines have passed.

_____ Does not coordinate work deadlines with other scheduling personnel whose work may affect these deadlines.

WORKING UNDER PRESSURE

Overall Rating

☐ Performance exceeds job standards—is beyond what is expected.

☐ Consistently good, competent, and proficient in meeting job standards.

☐ Does not meet job standards consistently. Performance in need of improvement.

☐ Not applicable or no opportunity to observe.

Examples of Behavior

_____ Works consistently under pressure without making a greater number of errors.

_____ Puts in overtime hours when needed.

_____ Helps out other employees in emergency work situation.

_____ Accepts changes in work assignments.

_____ Continues to meet required deadlines despite pressure.

_____ Works without additional supervision during stressful periods.

_____ Fails to follow through on work assignments under pressure.

_____ Constantly makes mistakes due to trying to work too fast.

_____ Absent frequently during high pressure periods.

_____ Does not accept changes in work assignments.

WORKING WITHOUT SUPERVISION

Overall Rating

Examples of Behavior

☐ Performance exceeds job standards—is beyond what is expected.

    _____ Takes responsibility and uses appropriate judgment to make changes in schedules that do not need supervisory review.

    _____ After completing regular work assignment, finds other tasks to perform without asking supervisory personnel.

    _____ Responds to problems that arise during a supervisor's absence without waiting for the supervisor's return.

☐ Consistently good, competent, and proficient in meeting job standards.

    _____ Performs assigned work without constantly referring to supervisory personnel for direction.

    _____ In a supervisor's absence will continue to work consistently.

    _____ Works without being constantly reminded by supervisory personnel.

    _____ Organizes daily workload; plans, lays out and sets up work without supervisor's assistance.

☐ Does not meet job standards consistently. Performance in need of improvement.

    _____ Will not take the initiative to make changes without supervisor's review and approval.

    _____ Will not perform additional work without being asked by supervisory personnel, even if he/she has completed regular assignment.

    _____ All work must be continually checked by the supervisor.

☐ Not applicable or no opportunity to observe.

GETTING ALONG WITH OTHERS

Overall Rating

☐ Performance exceeds job standards—is beyond what is expected.

☐ Consistently good, competent, and proficient in meeting standards.

☐ Does not meet job standards consistently. Performance in need of improvement.

☐ Not applicable or no opportunity to observe.

Examples of Behavior

_____ Deals very tactfully and helpfully with others.

_____ Goes out of the way to assist other employees in the section with work problems.

_____ Solicits comments from supervisory personnel regarding ways to improve work performance.

_____ When problems arise in dealing with other employees, works to resolve the situation.

_____ Accepts and implements constructive criticism and suggestions for work improvement.

_____ Cooperates with other staff.

_____ Uses tact in dealing with other employees.

_____ Will assist other employees with work when requested by supervisory personnel.

_____ Will not cooperate with other Section Personnel.

_____ Will not accept suggestions or constructive criticism about work performance.

_____ Gets defensive about work performance; often makes excuses.

_____ Will not assist other employees unless asked to do so by supervisory personnel.

Part II—Performance Development

In this section list those specific areas in which the employee has performed well. Include any outstanding examples of behavior that occurred during the rating period. Be sure to include accomplishments of objectives agreed to at the last performance appraisal. Attach any interim documentation (logs, memos, etc.) of critical incidents.

_____
_____
_____
_____
_____

Part III—Performance Development

In this section list those specific areas (from Part I) in which the employee needs to improve. Be sure to include objectives *not met* from last appraisal. Attach any interim documentation (logs, memos, etc.) of critical incidents.

_____
_____
_____
_____
_____

Part IV—Performance Objectives

In this section list specific objectives to improve performance during the next review period and actions to be taken to accomplish them. Be sure to address those areas listed in Part III.

Objective	Action to be Taken	Person to take Action

Part V—General Comments

In this section list any pertinent facts that should be known about the employee. For example, long illness or absence during the rating period, any special talents or skills that the employee has which may be used to advantage in other activities or positions, any recommendations you have, etc.

_____
_____
_____
_____

☐ Employee is performing satisfactorily and will be evaluated at the next regular performance evaluation session.

☐ Employee will be evaluated in _____ months because of unsatisfactory performance in the following areas:

_____
_____

Part VI—Employee Comments

In this section the employee should state any areas of concern or disagreement with his/her appraisal.

_____
_____
_____
_____

RATER'S SIGNATURE: _____ _____
                                                                                                                          DATE

EMPLOYEE'S SIGNATURE: _____ _____
(Your signature does not necessarily mean that you agree with the ratings.)   DATE

I WOULD LIKE TO DISCUSS THIS REPORT OR OTHER MATTERS WITH SOMEONE OTHER THAN MY RATING SUPERVISOR.

                    _____ YES   _____ NO

REVIEWER'S SIGNATURE: _____ _____
                                                                                                           DATE

APPENDIX

F

Customer/Client Appraisal Form

Appendix F represents a "customer/client appraisal" form used by one company to obtain feedback from customers and clients on the quality of the service they received.

MPS, Inc.

CUSTOMER SERVICE QUALITY SHEET

CUSTOMER NAME _____ TODAY'S DATE _____

ADDRESS _____ PHONE _____

_____ DATE OF SERVICE CALL _____

TO HELP US PROVIDE THE HIGHEST QUALITY SERVICE TO YOU AND TO OUR OTHER CUSTOMERS, WOULD YOU TAKE A FEW MINUTES TO COMPLETE THIS CUSTOMER SERVICE QUALITY SHEET. THANK YOU IN ADVANCE FOR YOUR HELP.

QUALITY OF SERVICE ___EXCELLENT ___GOOD ___OKAY ___FAIR ___UNSATISFACTORY

ATTITUDE OF SERVICEPERSON ___EXCELLENT ___GOOD ___OKAY ___FAIR ___UNSATISFACTORY

YES NO

___ ___ Did the serviceperson call to confirm the appointment?
___ ___ Did the serviceperson arrive within forty minutes of the scheduled time?
___ ___ Was the work neat with all material cleaned up?
___ ___ Were all of your questions answered?
___ ___ Do you understand how to operate the eqiupment that was installed?
___ ___ Was all the work that you have requested completed?
___ ___ If there were any unusual problems with the installation, did the serviceperson explain what the problems were?
___ ___ Did you receive a copy of the service call agreement?
___ ___ Were the service charges explained to you?
___ ___ Are you satisfied with the service?
___ ___ Would you like our customer service department to give you a call?

WHAT COMMENTS DO YOU HAVE?

_____
_____
_____
_____
_____
_____
_____
_____
_____

Glossary

Criterion—A criterion is a specific area of job performance upon which you will evaluate a subordinate's performance. Some other terms which can be used synonymously with criterion are: rating factor, job facet, performance factor, or job element. Some examples of criteria would include decision making ability, return on investment, typing ability, verbal communications, professional development, attendance, attention to detail, etc.

Job family—A group of jobs which have enough similarity to allow them to be grouped together for purposes of developing performance criteria.

Performance standard or expectation—A performance standard or expectation refers to the level of performance required within a criterion to receive a particular performance rating. For example, under the criterion of return on investment, there might be three performance standards to answer the three questions of: (1) What rate of return on investment would represent outstanding performance; (2) What rate of return on investment would represent satisfactory performance; and (3) What rate of return on investment would represent unsatisfactory performance? These definitions for levels of performance are sometimes referred to as behavioral anchors.

Reliability—Reliability refers to the consistency of a performance appraisal system.

Validity—Validity refers first of all to the degree to which the criteria in a performance appraisal system are related to the job of the person being evaluated and secondly to the degree to which the performance appraisal ratings actually reflect on-the-job performance.

Bibliography

Behaviorally Anchored Evaluations

Allan, P., and S. Rosenberg. "The Development of a Task-Oriented Approach to Performance Evaluation in the City of New York." *Public Personnel Management,* Vol 7 (1978), pp. 26–32.

Arvey, R., and J. Hoyle. "A Guttman Approach to the Development of Behaviorally Based Rating Scales for Systems Analysts and Programmer/analysts." *Journal of Applied Psychology,* Vol. 59 (1974), pp. 61–68.

Beatty, R., C. Schneier, and C. Beatty. "An Empirical Investigation of Perceptions of Ratee Behavior Frequency and Ratee Behavior Change Using Behavioral Expectation Scales (BES)." *Personnel Psychology,* Vol. 30 (1977), pp. 647–658.

Beer, M., and R. Ruh. "Employee Growth Through Performance Management." *Harvard Business Review,* Vol. 54 (1974), pp. 59–66.

Blood, M. "Spin-Offs From Behavioral Expectation Scale Procedures." *Journal of Applied Psychology,* Vol. 59 (1974), pp. 513–515.

Borman, W. "The Rating of Individuals in Organizations: An Alternate Approach." *Organizational Behavior and Human Performance,* Vol. 12 (1974), pp. 105–124.

Borman, W., and M. Dunnette. "Behavior-Based Versus Trait-Oriented Performance Ratings: An Empirical Study." *Journal of Applied Psychology,* Vol. 60 (1975), pp. 561–565.

Borman, W., and R. Vallon. "A View of What Can Happen When Behavioral Expectation Scales are Developed in One Setting and Used In Another." *Journal of Applied Psychology,* Vol. 59 (1974), pp. 197–201.

Campion, J., J. Greiner, and S. Wernli. "Work Observation Versus Recall in Developing Behavioral Examples for Rating Scales." *Journal of Applied Psychology,* Vol. 58 (1973), pp. 286–288.

Cascio, W., and E. Valenzi. "Relations Among Criteria of Police Performance." *Journal of Applied Psychology,* Vol. 63 (1978), pp. 22–28.

Dunnette, M., R. Arvey, and L. Hellervik. "The Development and Evaluation of Behaviorally Based Rating Scales." *Journal of Applied Psychology,* Vol. 57 (1973), pp. 15–22.

Finley, D., J. Dubin, and P. Jenneret. "Behaviorally Based Rating Scales: Effects of Specific Anchors and Disguised Scale Continua." *Personnel Psychology,* Vol. 30 (1977), pp. 659–669.

Goodale, J., and R. Burke. "Behaviorally-Based Rating Scales Need Not Be Job Specific." *Journal of Applied Psychology,* Vol. 60 (1975), pp. 389–391.

Ivancevich, J. "Expectancy Theory Predictions and Behaviorally Anchored Scales of Motivation: An Empirical Test of Engineers." *Journal of Vocational Behavior,* Vol. 8 (1976), pp. 59–75.

Kearney, W. "The Value of Behaviorally Based Performance Appraisal." *Business Horizons,* Vol. 19 (196-76), pp. 75–83.

Krauze, M., S. Zedeck, N. Imparato, and T. Oleno. "Development of Behaviorally Anchored Rating Scales as a Function of Organizational Level." *Journal of Applied Psychology,* Vol. 59 (1974), pp. 249–252.

Landy, F., J. Farr, F. Saal, and W. Freytag. "Behaviorally Anchored Scales for Rating the Performance of Police Officers." *Journal of Applied Psychology,* Vol. 61 (1976) pp. 750–758.

Latham, G., C. Fay, and L. Saari. "The Development of Behavioral Observation Scales for Appraising the Performance of Forman." *Personnel Psychology,* Vol. 32 (1979), pp. 299–311.

Latham, G., and K. Wexley. "Behavioral Observation Scales for Performance Appraisal Purposes." *Personnel Psychology,* Vol. 30 (1977), pp. 255–268.

Levinson, H. "Appraisal of *What* Performance?" *Harvard Business Review,* Vol. 50 (1972), pp. 30–33.

Schwab, D., H. Heneman, and T. Decotis. "Behaviorally Anchored Rating Scales: A Review of the Literature." *Proceeding of Academy of Management,* Vol. 18 (1975).

Smith, P., and L. Kendall. "Retranslation of Expectations: An Approach to the Construction of Unambiguous Anchors for Rating Scales." *Journal of Applied Psychology,* Vol. 47 (1963), pp. 149–155.

Taber, T., and J. Hackman. "Dimensions of Undergraduate College Performance." *Journal of Applied Psychology,* Vol. 61 (1976), pp. 546–558.

EEO

Froelich, H., and D. Hawver. "Compliance Spinoff: Better Personnel Systems." *Personnel,* Vol. 50 (1974), pp. 62–68.

Holley, W., and H. Field. "Performance Appraisal and the Law." *Labor Law Journal,* Vol. 26 (1975), pp. 423–430.

Holley, W., H. Field, and N. Barnett. "Analyzing Performance Appraisal Systems: An Empirical Study." *Personnel Journal,* Vol. 55 (1976), pp. 457–459.

Lubben, G. "Performance Appraisal: The Legal Implications of Title VII," *Personnel,* Vol. 57 (1980), pp. 11–21.

Schneier, D. "Impact of EEO Legislation on Performance Appraisal." *Personnel,* Vol. 55 (1978), pp. 24–34.

Schwab, D., and H. Heneman. "Research Round-Up." *Personnel Administrator,* January (1977), pp. 54–56.

Stanton, E. "The Discharged Employee and the EEO Laws." *Personnel Journal,* Vol. 55 (1976), pp. 128–129.

Effects of the Appraisal Systems

Cummings, L. "A Field Study of the Effects of Two Performance Appraisal Systems." *Personnel Psychology,* Vol. 26 (1973), pp. 489–502.

Davis, P. "Do They Agree With Your Appraisals of Their Performance?" *Supervisory Management,* Vol. 19 (1974), pp. 14–18.

Flowers, V. "Who Do You Think You're Talking To?" *Supervisory Management*, Vol. 22 (1977), pp. 14–24.

Hillery, J., and K. Wexley. "Participation Effects in Appraisal Interviews Conducted in a Training Situation." *Journal of Applied Psychology,* Vol. 2 (1974), pp. 168–171.

Ilgen, D., and J. Gunn. "Affective Consequences of Disconfirming Performance Expectations." *Journal of Social Psychology,* Vol. 100 (1976).

Konkel, G., and P. Peck. "How Subordinates Judge Word Processing Managers." *The Office,* Vol. 83 (1976), pp. 46–54.

Lee, M., and W. Ziverman. "Designing a Motivation and Team Building Employee Appraisal System." *Personnel Journal,* Vol. 55 (1976), pp. 354–357.

Liberman, A. "The Employee Service Review: Worker Perceptions of the System." *Public Personnel Management,* Vol. 6 (1977), pp. 84–90.

Massey, D. "Narrowing the Gap Between Intended and Existing Results of Appraisal Systems." *Personnel Journal,* Vol. 54 (1975), pp. 522–524.

Nisberg, J. "Performance Improvement Without Training." *Personnel Journal,* Vol. 55 (1976), pp. 613–615.

Schlesigner, L. "Performance Improvement: The Missing Component of Appraisal Systems." *Personnel Journal,* Vol. 55 (1976), pp. 274–275.

Sheridan, R., and R. Carlson. "Decision-Making in a Performance Appraisal Situation." *Personnel Psychology,* Vol 2 (1972), pp. 339–352.

Evaluation of Faculty and Administrators

Bernardin, J. "Behavioral Expectation Scales Versus Summated Scales: A Fairer Comparison." *Journal of Applied Psychology,* Vol. 62 (1977), pp. 422–427.

Bernardin, J., and C. Walter. "Effects of Rater Training and Diary-Keeping on Psychometric Error in Ratings." *Journal of Applied Psychology,* Vol. 62 (1977), pp. 64–69.

Braunstein, D., G. Klein, and M. Pachlo. "Feedback Expectancy and Shifts in Student Ratings of College Faculty." *Journal of Applied Psychology,* Vol. 58 (1973), pp. 254–258.

Burnaska, R., and T. Hollman "An Empirical Comparison of the Relative Effects of Rater Response Biases on Three Rating Scale Formats." *Journal of Applied Psychology,* Vol. 59 (1974), pp. 307–312.

Harari, O., and S. Zedeck. "Development of Behaviorally Anchored Scales for the Evaluation of Faculty Teaching." *Journal of Applied Psychology*, Vol. 58 (1973), pp. 261–265.

Hegarty, W. "Supervisors' Reaction to Subordinates' Appraisals." *Personnel*, Vol. 5 (1973), pp. 30–36.

Hegarty, W. "Using Subordinate Ratings to Elicit Behavioral Changes in Supervisors." *Journal of Applied Psychology,* Vol. 59 (1974), pp. 764–766.

Keaveny, T., and A. McGann. A Comparison of Behavioral Expectation Scales and Graphic Rating Scales." *Journal of Applied Psychology,* Vol. 60 (1975), pp. 695–703.

Merideth, G., and D. Bub. "Evaluation of Apprenticeship Teaching in Higher Education." *Psychological Reports,* Vol. 40 (1977), pp. 1123–1126.

Todd, D. "Job Evaluation Goes to School." *Personnel,* Vol. 51 (1974), pp. 53–59.

Feedback Systems

Arnold, H. "Effects of Performance Feedback and Extrinsic Reward Upon High Intrinsic Motivation." *Organizational Behavior and Human Performance,* Vol. 17 (1976), pp. 275–288.

Brickman, P., A. Linsemmeier, and W. McCareins. "Performance Enhancement by Relevant Success and Irrelevant Failure." *Journal of Personality and Social Psychology,* Vol. 33 (1976), pp. 149–160.

Clutterback, D. "Helping Managers Improve Performance Appraisal. "*International Management,* Vol. 31 (1976), pp. 41–46.

Dwyer, J., and N. Dimitroff. "The Bottoms Up/Tops Down Approach to Performance Appraisal." *Personnel Journal,* Vol. 55 (1976), pp. 349–353.

Dyer, W. "Encouraging Feedback." *Personnel Administrator,* June (1974).

Fisher, C. "Transmission of Positive and Negative Feedback to Subordinates: A Laboratory Investigation." *Journal of Applied Psychology,* Vol. 64 (1979), pp. 533–540.

Ford, R., and K. Jennings. "How to Make Performance Appraisals More Effective." *Personnel,* Vol. 2 (1977), pp. 51–56.

Graen, G., T. Minami, and J. Cashman. "Leadership Behaviors As Cues to Performance Evaluation." *Academy of Management Journal,* Vol. 16 (1973), pp. 611–635.

Halish, F., and H. Hechhausen. "Search for Feedback Information and Effort Regulation During Task Performance." *Personality and Social Psychology,* Vol. 35 (1977), pp. 724–733.

Heisler, W. "A Performance Correlate of Personal Control Beliefs in an Organizational Context." *Journal of Applied Psychology,* Vol. 59 (1974), pp. 504–506.

Herold, D., and M. Greller. "Feedback: The Definition of a Construct." *Academy of Management Journal,* Vol. 20 (1977), pp. 142–147.

Kippel, G. "Information Feedback Schedules, Interpolated Activities, and Retention." *Journal of Psychology,* Vol. 87 (1974), pp. 245–251.

Pelc, R., and E. Midlarsky. "Effects of Evaluative Feedback on the Subjective Probability of Success." *Journal of Psychology,* Vol. 96 (1977), pp. 191–196.

Quaglieri, P. "Feedback and Feedback." *Supervisory Management,* Vol. 25 (1980), pp. 34–38.

Ringer, W. "Frequent Reviews Improve Employee Relations." *Journal of Systems Management,* Vol. 26 (1975), pp. 26–37.

Sigall, H., and R. Gould. "The Effects of Self-Esteem and Evaluator Demandingness on Effort Expenditure." *Journal of Personality and Social Psychology,* Vol. 35 (1977), pp. 12–20.

General

Amidon, R., A. Arbeit, P. Liberman, and E. Williams. "Personal Evaluation—A Proposal for Employment Standards." *Public Personnel Management,* Vol. 4 (1975), pp. 248–258.

Back, K., and M. Horner. "Successful Schemes for Management Appraisal." *Personnel Management,* July (1973), pp. 30–33.

Bishop, T., and R. McKenna. "Getting Results From Performance Appraisals." *Infosystems,* Vol. 23 (1976), pp. 62–63.

Cohen, S., and L. Penner. "The Rigors of Predictive Validation: Some Comments on a Job Learning Approach to Performance Prediction." *Personnel Psychology,* Vol 29 (1976), pp. 595–600.

Colby, J., and R. Wallace. "The Art of Leveling with Subordinates About Their Performance." *Supervisory Management,* Vol. 20 (1975), pp. 26–29.

Decotis, T., and A. Petit. "The Performance Appraisal Process: A Model And Some Testable Propositions." *Academy of Management Review,* Vol. 3 (1978), pp. 635–646.

Ferrara, A. "Performance Appraisal: Steer Clear of Booby Traps." *Supervisory Management,* Vol. 20 (1975), pp. 2–9.

Fournies, F. "Why Management Appraisal Doesn't Help Develop Managers." *Management Review,* Vol. 63 (1974), pp. 19–24.

Hastings, R. "Examining Employee Evaluations." *Business Horizons,* Vol. 19 (1976), pp. 77–83.

Hayden, R. "Performance Appraisal: A Better Way." *Personnel Journal,* Vol. 7 (1973), pp. 606–613.

Hopkins, W. "Performance Appraisal: Try Action Analysis." *Supervisory Management,* Vol. 20 (1975), pp. 10–13.

Jacobs, A. "What's Wrong With Performance Appraisal Programs?" *Supervisory Management,* Vol. 22 (1977), pp. 10–15.

Kavanagh, M. "Put the Person Back in Performance Appraisal." *Supervisory Management,* Vol. 17 (1972), pp. 9–14.

Kearney, W. "Performance Appraisals: Which Way To Go? *MSU Business Topics,* Vol. 19 (1977), pp. 58–64.

Kindall, A., and J. Gatza. "Positive Program for Performance Appraisal." *Harvard Business Review,* Vol. 41 (1963), pp. 152–166.

Kreitner, R. "People Are Systems, Too: Filling the Feedback Vacuum." *Business Horizons,* Vol. 20 (1977), pp. 54–58.

Lazer, R., and W. Wikstrom. "Appraising Managerial Performance: Current Practices and Future Directions." *Across the Board,* Vol. 9 (1977).

Lloyd, W. "Performance Appraisals: A Shortsighted Approach for Installing a Workable Program." *Personnel Journal,* Vol. 56 (1977), pp. 446–450.

Locher, A., and K. Teel. "Performance Appraisal—A Survey of Current Practices." *Personnel Journal,* Vol. 56 (1977), pp. 245–247.

McAfee, B., and B. Green. "Selecting a Performance Appraisal Method." *Personnel Administrator,* June (1977), pp. 61–64.

McCoy, R. "Performance Review: Confronting the Poor Performer." *Supervisory Management,* Vol. 21 (1976), pp. 12–16.

McGregor, D. "An Uneasy Look at Performance Appraisal." *Harvard Business Review,* Vol. 35 (1957), pp. 89–94.

Meyer, H. "The Annual Performance Review Discussion—Making It More Constructive." *Personnel Journal,* Vol. 56 (1977), pp. 508–511.

Meyer, H. "The Science of Telling Executives How They're Doing." *Fortune,* Vol. LXXXX (1974), pp. 102–112.

Muse, A. "The Appraisal System." *C.A. Magazine,* Vol. 110 (1977), pp. 23–24.

Oberg, W. "Make Performance Appraisal Relevant." *Harvard Business Review,* Vol. 50 (1972), pp. 61–67.

Patz, A. "Performance Appraisal: Useful But Still Resisted." *Harvard Business Review,* Vol. 53 (1975), pp. 74–80.

Rieder, G. "Performance Review—A Mixed Bag." *Harvard Business Review,* Vol. 51 (1973), pp. 61–67.

Saleh, S. and J. Hosek. "Job Involvement: Concepts and Measurements." *Academy of Management Journal,* Vol. 19 (1976), pp. 213–233.

Salton, G. "VARIMAT: Variable Format Performance Appraisal." *Personnel Administrator,* June (1977), pp. 53–58.

Schwartz, D. "A Job Sampling Approach to Merit System Examining." *Personnel Psychology,* Vol. 30 (1977), pp. 175–185.

Silverman, R., and I. Menessa. "Employee Appraisal Systems." *Journal of Systems Management,* Vol. 27 (1976), pp. 36–38.

Stewart, A., and V. Stewart. "Selection and Appraisal: The Pick of Recent Research." *Personnel Management,* Vol. 8 (1976), pp. 20–24.

Talbert, T., K. Carroll, and W. Ronan. "Measuring Clerical Job Performance." *Personnel Journal,* Vol. 55 (1976), pp. 573–575.

Willcoxon, S., and C. Brocato. "Improving Results Through an Integrated Management System: A Case Study." *Management Review,* Vol. 65 (1976), pp. 18–27.

Williams, R., J. Walker, and C. Fletcher. "International Review of Staff Appraisal Practices." *Public Personnel Management,* Vol. 6 (1977), pp. 5–12.

Goal Setting

Connolly, T. "Some Conceptual and Methodological Issues in Expectancy Models of Work Performance Motivation." *Academy of Management Review,* Vol. 1 (1976), pp. 37–47.

Erez, M. "Feedback: A Necessary Condition for the Goal Setting-Performance Relationship." *Journal of Applied Psychology,* Vol. 62 (1977), pp. 62–65.

Hayes, M. "Do Appraisal Reviews Improve Performance?" *Public Personnel Management,* Vol. 2 (1973), pp. 128–133.

Heiger, H. "Implementing an Appraisal-by-Results Program." *Personnel,* Vol. 47 (1970), pp. 24–32.

Hughes, C. "Assessing The Performance of Key Managers." *Personnel,* Vol. 45 (1968), pp. 38–43.

Ivancevich, J. "Differing Goal Setting Treatments and Their Effects on Performance and Job Satisfaction." *Academy of Management Journal,* Vol. 20 (1977), pp. 406–419.

Kim, J., and W. Hamner. "Effect of Performance Feedback and Goal Setting on Productivity and Satisfaction in an Organizational Setting." *Journal of Applied Psychology,* Vol. 61 (1976), pp. 48–57.

Kirchhoff, B. "A Diagnostic Tool for Management by Objectives." *Personnel Psychology,* Vol. 28 (1975), pp. 351–364.

London, M., and G. Oldham. "Effects of Varying Goal Types and Incentive Systems on Performance and Satisfaction." *Academy of Management Journal*, Vol. 21 (1978), pp. 537–546.

Patton, T. "Linking Financial Rewards to Employee Performance: The Roles of OD and MBO." *Human Resources Management*, Winter, (1973).

Interviewing/Counseling

Dexter, J. "Can You Level With Your Subordinates?" *Supervisory Management*, Vol. 16 (1971), pp. 9–12.

Gould, M. "Counseling for Self-Development." *Personnel Journal*, Vol. 49 (1970), pp. 226–234.

Grandy, C. "Do Your Performance Appraisals Backfire?" *Supervisory Management*, Vol. 16 (1971) pp. 2–6.

Henry, J. "Are You Good At Career Counseling?" *Supervisory Management*, Vol. 19 (1974), pp. 22–27.

Klos, J. "Take The Pain Out of Performance Appraisal." *Supervisory Management*, Vol. 18 (1973), pp. 22–25.

Moorby, E. "The Manager as Coach." *Personnel Management*, Vol. 5 (1972), pp. 30–32.

Zawacki, R., and P. LaSota. "The Supervisor as Counselor." *Supervisory Management*, Vol. 18 (1973), pp. 16–20.

Management

Demski, J. "Uncertainty and Evaluation Based on Controllable Performance." *Journal of Accounting Research*, Autumn (1976).

Foster, C., D. Gustafson, and S. Norton. "How One Company Assesses Management Potential." *Personnel*, Vol. 50 (1973), pp. 48–56.

Howe, W. "Appraisal Systems Measure On-The-Job Effectiveness." *Administrative Management*, Vol. 37 (1977), pp. 26–30.

Koontz, H. *Managerial Appraisal*, New York, NY: McGraw-Hill, 1971.

Perham, J. "Pay Off In Performance Bonuses." *Dunn's Review*, May (1974), pp. 51–55.

Reese, C. "Executive Performance Appraisal-The View From the Top." *Personnel Journal*, Vol. 54 (1975), pp. 42–67.

Villareal, M. "Improving Managerial Performance." *Personnel Journal*, Vol. 56 (1977), pp. 86–89.

Winstanley, N. "Performance Appraisals and Management Development: A Systems Approach." *Conference Board Record*, Vol. 8 (1976), pp. 55–59.

Worbois, G. "Validation of Externally Developed Assessment Procedures for Identification of Supervisory Potential." *Personnel Psychology*, Vol. 28 (1975), pp. 77–91.

Motivation

Harrell, T.: *Industrial Psychology*, 1949. Rinehardt. New York.

Kopelman, R. "Merit Rewards, Motivation, and Job Performance." *Research Management*, Vol. XX (1977), pp. 25–37.

Krag, G.: *Personality Factors*, 1955. Funk and Wagnalls. New York.

Lee, M., and W. Zwerman. "Designing a Motivating and Team Building Employee Appraisal System." *Personnel Journal*, Vol. 7 (1976), pp. 354–357.

Maier, N.: *Supervisory and Executive Development.* 1957. Wiley. New York.

Manhardt, P. "The Effects of Managers' Performance Evaluation Policies on Subordinate Motivation in a Program of Management by Objectives." *Dissertation Abstracts International,* Vol. 38 (10–b) (1978), pp. 5079–5080.

Miner, J.: *Management of Ineffective Performance.* 1963. McGraw-Hill. New York.

Miner, J.: *Personnel Psychology.* 1969. MacMillan. New York.

Sayles, L.: *Human Behavior In Organizations.* 1966. Prentice Hall. New Jersey.

Todd, J. "Management Control Systems: A Key Link Between Strategy, Structure, and Employee Performance." *Organizational Dynamics,* Vol. 5 (1977), pp. 65–68.

VanDuren, A. "The Value of Performance Appraisal in the Motivation of Engineering Personnel." *Dissertation Abstracts International,* Vol. 37 (4–b) (1976), pp. 1954–1955.

Peer and Self Appraisal

Baird, L. "Self and Superior Ratings of Performance: As Related to Self-esteem and Satisfaction with Supervision." *Academy of Management Journal,* Vol. 20 (1977), pp. 291–300.

Denisi, A., and J. Mitchell. "An Analysis of Peer Ratings as Predictors and Criterion Measures and a Proposed New Application." *Academy of Management Review,* Vol. 3 (1978), pp. 369–374.

Denisi, A., and J. Shaw. "Investigation of the Uses of Self-Reports of Abilities." *Journal of Applied Psychology,* Vol. 62 (1977), pp. 641–644.

Farley J. "Peer Nominations Without Peers?" *Journal of Applied Psychology,* Vol. 61 (1976), pp. 109–111.

Greller, M. "Subordinate Participation and Reactions to the Appraisal Interview." *Journal of Applied Psychology,* Vol. 60 (1975), pp. 544–549.

Heneman, H. "Comparison of Self and Superior Ratings of Managerial Performance." *Journal of Applied Psychology,* Vol. 59 (1974), pp. 638–642.

Holzbach, R. "Rater Bias in Performance Ratings: Super, Self and Peer Ratings." *Journal of Applied Psychology,* Vol. 63 (1978), pp. 579–588.

Kaufman, G., and J. Johnson. "Scaling Peer Ratings." *Journal of Applied Psychology,* Vol. 59 (1974), pp. 302–306.

Klimoski, J., and M. Londen. "Role of the Rater in Performance Appraisal." *Journal Of Applied Psychology,* Vol. 4 (1974), pp. 445–451.

Kraut, A. "Comparison of Self and Superior Ratings of Managerial Performance." *Journal of Applied Psychology,* Vol. 59 (1974), pp. 638–642.

Kraut, A. "Prediction of Managerial Success by Peer and Training Staff Rating." *Journal of Applied Psychology,* Vol. 60 (1975), pp. 14–19.

Levine, E., A. Flory, and R. Ash. "Self-Assessment in Personnel Selection." *Journal of Applied Psychology,* Vol. 62 (1977), pp. 428–435.

Meser, W. "Peer Group Reviewers Favored by Survey Respondents." *Data Management,* Vol. 15 (1977), p. 28.

Olsen, L., and A. Bennett. "Performance Appraisal: Management Technique or Social Process?" *Management Review,* Vol. 1 (1976), pp. 22–28.

Orpen, C. "Peer Ratings as Predictors of White Collar Performance." *Personnel,* Vol. 49 (1972), pp. 45–49.

Police, Navy, NASA, ROTC, and Government/Public Employees

Casio, W., and V. Enzo. "Behaviorally Anchored Rating Scales: Effects of Education and Job Experience of Raters and Ratees." *Journal of Applied Psychology,* Vol. 62 (1977), pp. 278–282.

Craver, G. "Survey of Job Evaluation Practices in State and County Government." *Public Personnel Management,* Vol. 6 (1977), pp. 121–131.

DeCotis, T. "An Analysis of the External Validity and Applied Relevance of Three Rating Formats." *Organizational Behavior and Human Performance,* Vol. 19 (1977), pp. 247–266.

Downey, R., E. Medland, and L. Yates. "Evaluation of a Peer Rating System for Predicting Subsequent Promotion of Senior Military Officers." *Journal of Applied Psychology,* Vol. 61 (1976), pp. 206–209.

Feldaus, J. "Weighted Ratings: Performance Criteria for Concurrent Validations of a Police Selection Test." *Public Personnel Management,* Vol. 5 (1976)

Field, H., and W. Holley. "Traits in Performance Ratings—Their Importance in Public Employment." *Public Personnel Management,* Vol. 4 (1975), pp. 327–330.

Githens, W., R. Eister, G. Musgrove, and J. Crieghton. "Personnel Development and Evaluation." *Omega,* Vol. 4 (1976), pp. 341–342.

Holley, W., and H. Field. "Performance Appraisal—An Analysis of State-wide Practices." *Public Personnel Management,* Vol. 4 (1975), pp. 145–150.

Keeley, M. "Subjective Performance Evaluation and Person-Role Conflict Under Conditions of Uncertainty." *Academy of Management Journal,* Vol. 20 (1977), pp. 315–321.

Millard, C., F. Luthans, and R. Otteman. "A New Breakthrough for Performance Appraisal." *Business Horizons,* Vol. 19 (1976), pp. 66–73.

Mullett, G., W. Ronan, and T. Talbert. "Prediction of Job Performance Dimensions: Police Officers." *Public Personnel Management,* Vol. 6 (1977), pp. 173–180.

Rizzo, W., and F. Frank. "Influence of Irrelevant Cues and Alternate Forms of Graphic Rating Scales on the Halo Effect." *Personnel Psychology,* Vol. 30 (1977), pp. 415–417.

Saal, F. and F. Landy. "The Mixed Standard Rating Scale: An Evaluation." *Organizational Behavior and Human Performance,* Vol. 19 (1977), pp. 19–35.

Siegal, A., and B. Bergman. "A Job Training Approach to Performance Prediction." *Personnel Psychology,* Vol. 28 (1975), pp. 325–339.

Tavernier, G. "Public Servants Rate their Own Performance." *International Management,* Vol. 32 (1977), pp. 19–21.

Taylor, R., and R. Zawacki. "Collaborative Goal Setting in Performance Appraisal." *Public Personnel Management,* Vol. 7 (1978), pp. 162–170.

Webb, G. "National Job Evaluation in the Current Climate." *Personnel Management,* Vol. 5 (1973), pp. 29–31.

Rater-Ratee Characteristics

Bensahel, J. "Do You Hate to Criticize?" *International Management,* Vol. 28 (1973), pp. 32–34.

Borman, W. "Effects of Instructions to Avoid Halo Error on Reliability and Validity of Performance Evaluation Ratings." *Journal of Applied Psychology,* Vol. 60 (1975), pp. 556–560.

Chambers, P. "Teaching Managers How to Interview." *International Management,* Vol. 28 (1973), pp. 41–43.

Cowan, J. "A Human Factored Approach to Appraisals." *Personnel,* Vol. 52 (1975), pp. 49–56.

Friedman, B., and E. Cornelius. "Effect of Rater Participation in Scale Constrution on the Psychometric Characteristics of Two Rating Scale Formats." *Journal of Applied Psychology,* Vol. 61 (1976), pp. 210–216.

Jenkins, G., D. Nadler, E. Lawler, and C. Cammann. "Standardized Observations—An Approach to Measuring the Nature of Jobs." *Journal of Applied Psychology,* Vol. 60 (1975), pp. 171–181.

Latham, G., K. Wexley, and E. Pursell. "Training Managers to Minimize Rating Errors in the Observation of Behavior." *Journal of Applied Psychology,* Vol. 60 (1975), pp. 550–555.

Miller, L. "Errors in Performance Rating as a Function of Supervisor/Subordinate Situational Characteristics and Job Content Agreement." *Dissertation Abstracts International,* Vol. 37 (11–B) (1977), p. 5816.

Overman, R. "The Effects of Rater-Ratee Similarity on Rated Job Performance as a Function of the Rating Instrument." *Dissertation Abstracts/International,* Vol. 38 (7–B) (1978), p. 3450.

Pizam, A. "Social Differentiation—A New Psychological Barrier to Performance Appraisal." *Public Personnel Journal,* Vol. 4 (1975), pp. 244–247.

Pursell, E., D. Dossett, and G. Latham. "Obtaining Valid Predictors by Minimizing Rating Errors in the Criterion." *Personnel Psychology,* Vol. 33 (1980), pp. 91–96.

Schmidt, N. "Interrater Agreement in Dimensionality and Combination of Assessment Center Judgements." *Journal of Applied Psychology,* Vol. 62 (1977), pp. 171–176.

Schneier, C. "Multiple Rater Groups and Performance Appraisal." *Public Personnel Management,* Vol. 6 (1977), pp. 13–20.

Schneier, C., and R. Beatty. "The Influence of Role Prescription on the Performance Appraisal Process." *Academy of Management Journal,* Vol. 21 (1978), pp. 129–135.

Wagner, R. "Generalizability of Position Error in Ranking." *Psychological Reports,* Vol. 37 (1975), pp. 811–814.

Sex, Race, and Other Biases

Bartol, K., and D. Butterfield. "Sex Effects in Evaluating Leaders." *Journal of Applied Psychology,* Vol. 61 (1976), pp. 446–454.

Bigoness, W. "Effects of Applicant's Sex, Race and Performance Ratings: Some Additional Findings." *Journal of Applied Psychology,* Vol. 61 (1976), pp. 80–84.

Brief, A., and M. Wallace. "The Impact of Employee Sex and Performance on the Allocation of Organizational Rewards." *Journal of Psychology,* Vol. 92 (1976), pp. 25–34.

Deaux, D., and T. Emswiller. "Explanation of Successful Performance on Sex-Linked Tasks: What is Skill for the Male is Luck for the Female." *Journal of Personality and Social Psychology,* Vol. 29 (1974), pp. 80–85.

Feather, N., and J. Simon. "Reactions to Male and Female Success and Failure in Sex Linked Occupations: Impressions of Personality, Causal Attributes, and Perceived Likelihood of Different Consequences." *Journal of Personality and Social Psychology,* Vol. 31 (1975), pp. 20–31.

Gallagher, M. "More Bias in Performance Evaluation?" *Personnel,* Vol. 55 (1978), pp. 35–40.

Greenberg, J. "The Protestant Work Ethic and Reactions to Negative Performance Evaluations on a Laboratory Task." *Journal of Applied Psychology,* Vol. 62 (1977).

Grey, R., and D. Kipnis. "Untangling the Performance Appraisal Dilemma: The Influence of Perceived Organizational Context on Evaluation Processes." *Journal of Applied Psychology,* Vol. 3 (1976), pp. 329–335.

Hamner, W., J. Kim, L. Baird, and W. Bigoness. "Race and Sex as Determinates of Rating by Potential Employees in a Simulated Work-Sample Task." *Journal of Applied Psychology,* Vol. 59 (1974), pp. 705–711.

Jacobson, M., and W. Koch. "Women as Leaders: Performance Evaluation as a Function of Method of Leader Selection." *Organizational Behavior and Human Performance,* Vol. 20 (1977), pp. 149–157.

Johnson, S., and L. Ronan. "Exploratory Study of Bias in Job Performance Evaluation." *Public Personnel Management,* Vol. 8 (1979), pp. 315–323.

Latham, G., K. Wexley, and E. Pursell. "Training Managers to Minimize Rating Errors in the Observation of Behavior." *Journal of Applied Psychology,* Vol. 60 (1975), pp. 550–555.

Lazer, R. "The Discrimination Danger in Performance Appraisal." *The Conference Board Record,* Vol. 8 (1976), pp. 60–64.

Lee, M., and K. Alvares. "Effects of Sex on Descriptions and Evaluations of Supervisory Behavior in a Simulated Industrial Setting." *Journal of Applied Psychology,* Vol. 4 (1977), pp. 405–410.

London, M., and J. Poplawski. "Effects of Information on Stereotype Development in Performance Appraisal and Interview Context." *Journal of Applied Psychology,* Vol. 61 (1976), pp. 199–205.

Nieva, V., and B. Gutek. "Sex Effects on Evaluation." *Academy of Management Review,* Vol. 5 (1980), pp. 267–276.

Outtz, J. "Racial Bias as a Contaminant of Performance Evaluation." *Dissertation Abstracts International,* Vol. 38 (5–B) (1977), p. 2414.

Rose, G. "Sex Effects on Effort Attributions in Managerial Performance Evaluation." *Organizational Behavior and Human Performance,* Vol. 21 (1978), pp. 367–378.

Rose, G., and T. Stone. "Why Good Job Performance May (not) be Rewarded—Sex Factors and Career Development." *Journal of Vocational Behavior,* Vol. 12 (1978), pp. 197–202.

Rosen, B., and T. Jerdee. "Influence of Sex-role Stereotypes on Personnel Decisions." *Journal of Applied Psychology,* Vol. 59 (1974), pp. 9–14.

Schmidt, N., and T. Hill. "Sex and Race Composition of Assessment Center Groups as a Determinant of Peer and Assessor Ratings." *Journal of Applied Psychology,* Vol. 62 (1977), pp. 261–264.

Scott, R. "Taking Subjectivity Out of Performance Appraisal." *Personnel,* Vol. 4 (1973), pp. 45–49.

Taynor, J., and K. Deux. "When Women Are More Deserving than Men: Equity, Attribution, and Perceived Sex Differences." *Journal of Personality and Social Psychology,* Vol. 28 (1973), pp. 360–367.

Webster, M., and D. Entwisle. "Expectation Effects on Performance Evaluations." *Social Forces,* Vol. 55 (1976), pp. 493–502.

Books on Performance Appraisal

Cummings, L. L. and Schwab, D. P. *Performance in Organizations: Determinants and Appraisal.* Glenview, IL: Scott, Foresman, and Company, 1973.

Dailey, C. A. and Madsen, A. M. *How to Evaluate People in Business.* New York, NY: McGraw-Hill, 1980.

Johnson, R. G. *The Appraisal Interview Guide.* New York, NY: AMACOM, 1979.

Latham, G. P. and Wexley, K. N. *Increasing Productivity through Performance Appraisal.* Reading, MA: Addison-Wesley Publishing Company, 1981.

Lefton, R. E., Buzzotta, V. R., Sherberg, M., and Karraker, D. L. *Effective Motivation through Performance Appraisal.* New York, NY: Wiley, 1977.

Kellogg, M. S. *What to Do About Performance Appraisal.* New York, NY: AMACOM, 1965.

Sloma, R. S. *How to Measure Managerial Performance.* New York, NY: Macmillan Publishing Company, 1980.